British Birds

in Colour

Bullfinches, cock (left) and hen, perching on a larch branch.

British Birds
in Colour

Advisory Editor: R. S. R. FITTER

Contributors

PHILIP E. BROWN · BRUCE CAMPBELL
R. M. LOCKLEY · E. R. PARRINDER
RICHARD PERRY

Illustrated with 108 plates in colour from
JOHN GOULD'S *The Birds of Great Britain*

Photographs by
E. J. HOSKING · G. K. YEATES
and others

Odhams Press Ltd   Long Acre, London

222

Merlin at nest with eggs.

CONTENTS

COLOUR PLATES

THE COLOUR PLATES which appear in this book are reproductions from John Gould's well-known work *The Birds of Great Britain*, which was published in 1873. Born in 1804 at Lyme Regis, Gould started work at the age of fourteen in the garden of Windsor Castle, and it was here that he first became interested in wild life. His interest soon led him to the art of stuffing birds and so skilled did he become that in 1827 he secured the post of taxidermist at the Museum of the newly formed Zoological Society of London. Two years later he married Miss E. Coxon, an artist, who assisted him in his work by drawing plates from his sketches. His first book, published in 1832, depicted birds of the Himalayas, and was by far the most accurately illustrated work on foreign ornithology that had appeared up to that time. In 1838 Gould and his wife sailed to Australia to study the natural life there. After an expedition lasting two years in this as yet unsettled continent, they published seven volumes illustrating the birds of Australia, with no less than six hundred coloured plates. By now Gould was regarded as a foremost authority on his subject and was rewarded in 1843 by being elected Fellow of the Royal Society. This, unfortunately, was a success that his wife could not share, for she had died two years before. Some twenty years later, in 1862, *The Birds of Great Britain* was begun and this has been described as "exhibiting the perfection of his work." Published in seven massive volumes, it was, owing to the costly methods of production existing in those days, within the range of the pockets of only a few, but Gould, who died eight years later, wrote in the Introduction, "It will scarcely be presumptuous in me to foretell that a period is not far distant when our native birds will be far more familiarly known to people than they are now." It is hoped that this book will further that wish of over half a century ago.

Mass flight of starlings photographed in the evening.

8

The pleasures of bird-watching

These his pursuits, by keeping the body and mind employed, have, under Providence, contributed to much health and cheerfulness of spirits, even to old age:—and, what still adds to his happiness, have led him to the knowledge of a circle of gentlemen whose intelligent communications, as they have afforded him much pleasing information, so, could he flatter himself with a continuation of them, would they ever be deemed a matter of singular satisfaction and improvement.

GILBERT WHITE, *The Natural History of Selborne*, 1788.

I N THESE and other beautifully written sentences the shy and retiring Gilbert White unconsciously established his reputation as the first English observer to record intelligently the pleasures and rewards of bird-watching. Writing to the Hon. Daines Barrington in 1771, he drew attention to the tendency of the naturalists of his day to content themselves with bare descriptions of dead birds, examined in the comfort of their armchairs, and declared that "the investigation of the life and conversation of animals is a concern of much more trouble and difficulty and is not to be attained but by the active and inquisitive, and by those that reside much in the country." White himself hardly moved out of his remote country parish, yet he discovered far more about the lives of the birds than did the (then more famous) naturalist Pennant, to whom he wrote that "my little intelligence is confined to the narrow sphere of my own observations at home." Yet he was able to correct some of Pennant's erroneous statements gathered from second-hand information. For the chief pleasure of bird-watching perhaps is that it can be enjoyed almost anywhere and at any time, and more can be discovered by steady observation at home than by rushing from one place to another in search of the rarer species. Yet if we have to travel, or have of necessity to live much in towns, birds are always with us. The traveller can watch them from car or train, the sailor sees gull and petrel circling his ship, the townsman has his sparrows and a surprising number of other kinds of birds in city parks, and even the night-watchman may learn something about the habits of owls.

People become bird-watchers in the first place because they experience pleasure in seeing the living bird, whose actions so often appear akin to those of human beings. In the majority of us this pleasurable interest begins when we are very young, and it involuntarily deepens as the mind grows in its capacity for aesthetic feeling. We delight more and more in the beautiful colours, the harmonious songs, the airy freedom of the flight of birds. Some of us remain content at this level, because we are unable or unwilling to spare the time necessary for more serious and scientific study. The older observers were born as it were by accident to bird-watching; that is to say, they received no training in the serious study of birds at school as they did, for example, in the study of arithmetic and grammar. Ornithology is a comparatively new subject in the educational world, although in America it has now reached the dignity of the university chair. In Britain, however, bird-study remains almost entirely in the category of a hobby; there are extremely few paid posts, either occupied or available, in ornithology.

There is a great joy and a depth of freedom in bird-watching which is perhaps not found in the same measure in allied studies such as botany, entomology, and geology, which require special equipment and necessitate the collection of specimens. The bird-watcher need have little apparatus—he is complete with only a notebook and field-glasses. Gone are the days of the gun and glass case. Bird-watching has become a bloodless sport, in which the observer uses all his skill to stalk his quarry, his mind active to interpret the movements and voices of birds, and to avoid their recognition of him as an enemy.

Since in Britain bird-watching is principally a hobby, there are many who feel that they cannot go beyond this stage of recognizing the common resident and migratory birds of their neighbourhood, about which species it is popularly supposed that everything of importance is already known. But this is a false assumption. A careful reading of the life-history summaries of British birds which can be found in the leading handbooks reveals that although much has been learned a great deal more remains to be observed. Recent monographs, even of so common a bird as the robin, have brought home to us that, even after the years of patient study which these books represent, there remains a crop of unanswered questions, as well as many new problems which arise inevitably from the discoveries published therein. Those who begin their bird-watching in towns will soon realize, for example, how little is known of the ubiquitous house-sparrow.

The more ardent watcher, not content merely to recognize the common birds of his town, village, or garden, will gradually pass through the pleasant stages of identifying the more uncommon species, and of adding (for him, fresh) species to his lists for his district and county. There is a wonderful

satisfaction in solving with certainty at last, by some characteristic peculiar to the species, the identity of the mysterious bird which has sung sweetly in some thicket or clump of reeds, or which has flown across our path in a certain spot each day. As the list of birds definitely recognized grows, confidence and enthusiasm increase. Soon we learn the delights, subtle but inwardly satisfying, of identifying a bird not only by its plumage but, while it is too far away for us to distinguish its colours, by its size, form or flight, or by its habit of creeping through a hedge or of climbing a tree in a certain manner. And we are able at last to recognize a bird without seeing it, merely by hearing its call-note.

The earlier bird-watchers had few books and no organization to assist them. Their writings sometimes show that when they came up against unsolved problems of behaviour they were content to write these off, in lofty terms, as part of the inscrutable Will of God. Some of these questions which were once considered divine mysteries have since been, at any rate partially, solved by modern observers, either working on their own or in groups. The lone ornithologist who refuses to work with others is a rarer phenomenon today; where he exists he is rather a pathetic figure, losing much through the lack of the warmth of human company, and the generous sharing of trust and knowledge. This does not mean, however, that the bird-watcher must never be alone, but rather that he should share the results of his solitary watching with others, by joining an organization and sending contributions to its publications.

The observer who lives in a remote country district, as did Gilbert White, may have little chance of meeting fellow enthusiasts, but he can keep in touch with the latest reports and discoveries by becoming a member of a national body such as the Royal Society for the Protection of Birds (if his inclination is largely aesthetic), or the British Trust for Ornithology (if he is interested in scientific studies). These two bodies have recently made

Group of knot with one bar-tailed godwit and oyster-catchers in the background.

recommendations designed to help the newcomer. The young beginner is advised to join the R.S.P.B. first and through them learn the importance of conserving birds, by avoiding the collecting of eggs, and by the provision of sanctuaries and reserves for the rare species; there is an attractive "Bird and Tree Scheme" which encourages bird-study through the schools. On leaving school the keen young watcher is advised to join the B.T.O. and take part in its various scientific inquiries, census work, its meetings, and to make use, so far as is practicable, of the central library situated at Oxford.

In addition to joining these national societies, the bird-watcher should support a local natural history society. The annual records of local societies are always worth examining and may save the new member much valuable time by providing him with local information as to the distribution of birds, enabling him to develop his work from a more advanced position than he had expected. The meetings of such societies are a pleasant social occasion, too: discussions, addresses of scientific interest, the exhibition of photographs, films, and sketches, and local rambles provide a background for new friendships. There will be some ardent observers who will find in the meetings of the local society a stimulus to study and leadership. Others, a little more diffident about their powers of observation, will prefer to follow the elected officers. Recently there has almost been a danger, in the rapid increase in the number and membership of these societies, that initiative may be lost and humility be too humble, from a lack of leaders and an overplus of followers. This danger is perhaps inherent in modern society, and it should be combated; the increase of leisure has brought great opportunities for study, but at the same time the provision of modern conveniences and comforts has resulted in a corresponding

Barn-owl with vole. The barn-owl feeds mainly on rodents and is very useful to the farmer.

Hen Montagu's harrier alighting on the nest with food for its young.

unwillingness to pioneer and face the hardships by which the more advanced studies are attained. We are too apt to look for a switch or a lever to do the job for us, to have the song of the nightingale relayed to us by radio, and the nesting of the great crested grebe televised for us; we leave too much to the leaders, to the other members of our society, and forget the joys of personal achievement which are relatively much more important.

Nevertheless organized bird-watching is popular. It is a natural development and it has come to stay, whether we like it or not. It is assuming many forms. Apart from the activities of local natural history societies, there are several nation-wide inquiries on foot. One of the first of these was organized by the Royal Society for the Protection of Birds: this was a census of the numbers and distribution of the barn-owl. Since then the British Trust for Ornithology has been responsible for or connected with all similar national ornithological inquiries, or, as they

Common tern by its nesting hollow in sand-dunes.

are called, field investigations. These provide stimulating opportunities for the bird-watcher who will both learn and contribute in one operation. Among those birds which have been or are being studied on this country-wide scale are the woodcock, heron, great crested grebe, rook, wood-pigeon, gannet, and fulmar petrel.

The aim of the British Trust for Ornithology is to promote both individual and co-operative research. Its three principal sub-committees deal respectively with research, the ringing of birds by means of which their movements can be determined, and the co-ordination of the work of the bird observatories—all closely related activities.

What is a bird observatory? The man who spends his leisure hours gratifying his intellec-

tual curiosity by watching and recording the habits of the birds in his garden or in his favourite wood, or on common or lake familiar to him, may be said to have established successfully a bird observatory. There are thousands of such private observatories all over the world. But in Britain and in Europe generally, the term Bird Observatory (in capital letters at any rate) is today used to denote a station specially set up with suitable apparatus for catching and ringing birds, and usually with living quarters provided for observers. Such stations, of which there are now several in Britain, are maintained by local societies, and are open to all genuine students of birds.

The North Sea island of Heligoland contained the first bird observatory of world-wide fame. Heinrich Gätke, living on this island at the time it was a British possession, immortalized its long list of birds in his book, *Heligoland as an Ornithological Observatory*, which was published in Britain in 1895. It was from the nets and artificial coverts set up by the Heligolanders to catch migratory birds that the idea of the first large bird-ringing traps originated. The term "Heligoland trap" is still used today to describe the large funnel-shaped wire-netting enclosures which have been erected at British observatories.

The first of these was built in 1933 on the bare, windswept island of Skokholm, off the coast of South Wales. It was erected in the garden of the only house on the island, as this provided the sole cover for the many hundreds of small woodland- and bush-loving birds which passed through the island on their autumn, winter, and spring migrations. As these birds swarmed into the garden it was not difficult to drive most of them down towards the narrow end of the funnel of netting, and so into a box placed under a pane of clear glass, against which they fluttered. Each captured bird was taken into the "ringing room," where it was identified, examined for sex, age, parasites, moult, etc., weighed, and then released after an aluminium ring had been placed on its leg. These rings, issued by the B.T.O., bear the address of the British Museum (Natural History), London, and, of course, an identifying number.

In the next year the Midlothian Ornithological Club established a Heligoland trap on the Isle of May in the Firth of Forth, and operated it successfully until the outbreak of the Second World War, when both observatories closed down. But an excellent start had been made, and at the end of the war they were re-opened, the old traps repaired and new ones built. Skokholm was taken over by the West Wales Field Society, and the Isle of May by a joint committee of the Midlothian Club and the Scottish Universities. Stimulated by these successes, other societies have opened observatories at strategic points elsewhere along the coast of Britain. Thus Fair Isle now has a Heligoland trap, with a competent ornithologist to supervise the ringing work. At Spurn Head the Yorkshire

Grey wagtail satisfying the voracious appetite of a young cuckoo.

Naturalists' Union has opened a migratory bird-ringing station with a large Heligoland trap, and a cottage to accommodate visitors. The Lundy Field Society has built a trap on Lundy Island off the north coast of Devon. Other ringing stations are contemplated or in preparation, not only on the coast, but at points inland: lately, at Gibraltar Point in Lincolnshire, a new bird-migration station has been set up, and made an encouraging start in the first season by ringing some rarities. Still more recently, an observatory has been opened at Clay, in Norfolk, near the famous bird sanctuary at Blakeney Point.

At some observatories, such as Skokholm and Fair Isle, a resident warden is provided who supervises the ringing and research work. At other stations, as at the Isle of May and Spurn Head, there is no resident warden.

Island observatories provide a delightful holiday for the bird-watcher. There is great beauty in the wide sea and sky, and the summer flowers which cover these islands. There are vast numbers of breeding sea-birds which can be studied, as well as the birds of passage caught in the ringing traps. Each island station has its gulls and auks. At Skokholm there are Manx shearwaters and storm-petrels as special birds not found plentifully at the other observatories. Lundy has buzzards and small land birds, the Isle of May has terns, and Fair Isle has fulmar petrels and skuas. The visitor can take his part in carrying out the long-term survey which is being made of these species, and he learns new methods and the latest technique. Persistent ringing of generations of birds, including the use of coloured rings for quick identification in the field, is yielding valuable information. At Skokholm, for example, it is found that marked Manx shearwaters visit Lundy Island in their night wanderings, a distance of forty miles, and they may feed six hundred miles from the nest in which their mate is incubating the solitary egg.

Distinct from bird observatories are the field-study centres recently established by the Council for the Promotion of Field Studies in widely different types of country in Suffolk, Yorkshire, Surrey, and Pembrokeshire. These embrace all branches of outdoor study, including ornithology. Their main objects are the provision of accommodation and facilities for short courses in practical field study under qualified teachers. University students are especially catered for, but individual research is also encouraged, and the lone bird-watcher welcomed.

Finally there are the duck decoys which have been converted from their former utilitarian use, as sources of food supply, to the scientific purpose of ringing. At the moment only two are functioning as bird-marking stations: that of Orielton in Pembrokeshire, and that of Slimbridge in Gloucestershire.

At Slimbridge, Mr. Peter Scott has built up a waterfowl observatory, which is now managed by the Severn Wildfowl Trust. There is a duck decoy, as well as a large collection of wild ducks and geese breeding in enclosures well provided with water and cover. But the greatest pleasure which the bird-watcher will get on his visit to this station during the winter will be the sight of hundreds of wild geese of various species grazing tranquilly within a few yards of the observer, who is concealed in one of several thatched huts erected along the edge of the saltings. Huts such as these formerly concealed men interested in killing these geese; now they are used by watchers who study the live fowl, and the geese grow more and more tame with this winter-long protection.

For so many years has man taken ruthless toll of the wild birds that several species have become extinct or very rare and in many parts of Europe today this extermination still goes on. Britain now leads the way in the new enthusiasm for bird protection and bird-study in the field, and as a result, in the last few years, rare species such as the avocet, bittern, marsh-harrier, and golden eagle are returning to breed in British haunts from which persecution in the last century drove them.

Pair of starlings in breeding plumage, with young.

Magpie perching on a spruce branch.

The technique of bird-watching

THE only essentials in bird-watching in its simplest form are a curious mind, an observant eye, a keen ear, and a retentive memory, assisted by an authoritative bird book with coloured plates. The pioneer naturalists of the seventeenth and eighteenth centuries, indeed, had to rely mainly on skins and stuffed specimens as aids to identification.

There is still no better training for a field naturalist than to serve his initial apprenticeship without further aids to observation. True you will not, with the naked eye, be able to determine the colouring of small birds in dark woods: therefore you must learn their call-notes and identify them by ear alone. You will have similar difficulty with birds in flight: therefore you must learn to recognize them by their shape and manner of flight. Distances at sea and on nesting cliffs are often great, but under such conditions you will identify many of the birds you see by the special technique they employ in diving, by whether they swim alone or in large "rafts" and, again, by flight; while on the cliffs, you will discover that certain species occupy certain parts of the cliff-face, some in solitary niches, some massed together in hundreds.

Since, presumably, watching birds is to be your relaxation and hobby—for there are fewer than a dozen professional ornithologists in Great Britain—you are under no obligation to begin the hard way; but it is a mistake to suppose that ornithology is a rich man's hobby requiring a mass of expensive equipment. On the contrary, there is none

cheaper, and if you care to begin with no equipment you stand a very good chance of being the better naturalist. With nothing to assist you in your observations, you will be forced to employ eye, ear, and field-craft to the greatest possible extent, both in identifying and watching your subject, until recognition becomes a matter almost of intuition.

Similarly, you are under no obligation to carry a notebook with you, in which to enter details of your observations for the benefit of science. Bird-watching should be a pleasure, rather than a duty. Most ornithologists, however, find additional pleasure in keeping notes, for there are always new observations to be made about birds, and even the beginner can contribute valuable notes on such matters as habitats and regional distribution. As to whether you use a cheap notebook or an expensive card-index for this purpose is for you to decide. Both are in use among all sorts and conditions of naturalists.

Naturally, a time will come when you feel that to gain the maximum enjoyment from watching birds you must have a pair of binoculars, which will enable you to obtain the closest possible view of your elusive quarry. Here a warning must be given. Before the war a really good pair of binoculars could be bought secondhand for a few pounds. Today there is a mass of worthless material on the market, both cheap and expensive. Bad binoculars are worse than useless, for not only is their magnification almost nil and their field of vision narrow, but they also distort size and colour in the most grotesque manner. It is a mistake to suppose, however, that the largest and most expensive binoculars are the best for the job. On the contrary, those enormous glasses with coated lenses and other modern devices are not suitable for a naturalist's general-purpose binoculars. Most of them are an intolerable weight, both to handle and to wear slung round one's neck—which is the proper place to wear binoculars, for birds do not wait while you remove your binoculars from their case—and all of them require careful handling, and protection from the wet.

By all means keep a luxury pair of glasses, though they add, of course, to the weight of one's gear—which is always a factor to be considered when a long day's bird-watching is contemplated. But for stock purposes a medium-sized pair of prismatic binoculars with a magnification of 6x or 8x and a field of vision of twenty-four or thirty-two diameters is the ideal glass. They are sufficiently powerful to cover any distance likely to be met with in normal bird-watching and, at the same time, bring up the image sharply and reveal the colours of plumage in dark places such as woods and the interior of bushes.

For coast and hill work it is useful to possess a modern telescope of the type which has about a 20x magnification and gives a two-inch objective. It is always a thrill to pick up the colours of a bird several miles distant on some reef or skerry; but for general purposes an instrument of this kind must be regarded as a luxury.

What points does one look for in identifying a bird by sight? At a distance, its silhouette and manner of flight: the swan with its extremely long neck stretched out straight in flight, but forming an S-shaped curve when the bird is at rest; the swooping flight, in long dipping bounds, of the woodpeckers and the mistle-thrush; the soaring song-flight of the sky-lark; the V-shaped flight formations of geese and ducks and sometimes gulls; the triangular-shaped wings of starlings; the rolling walk of rooks.

Under favourable conditions, and when conspicuous, size and colour may also be a means of distinguishing a bird—the great height and immensely long legs of the fishing heron; the canary-yellow rump of the green woodpecker, suddenly revealed as it swoops up to a tree from an ant-hill, and the snowy-white rump of a bullfinch; the black-tipped wings of the great dazzling white gannet; the very long, graduated tail of the black-and-white magpie.

At closer range one looks for the small but immediately distinctive points—the different-coloured specula on the wings of ducks; the minute size and yellow crown of the gold-crest; the robin's red breast; the redstart's flame-coloured tail; the hedge-sparrow's "shuffling" wings; the lapwing's long, curved crest. With the exception of those belonging to such families as the warblers, nearly every bird possesses some small difference in plumage or habit which one learns to recognize at a glance: but in nearly every case, too, its call-note or song is an invaluable aid to identity.

With your binoculars and notebook you can consider yourself adequately equipped. It may be useful to carry

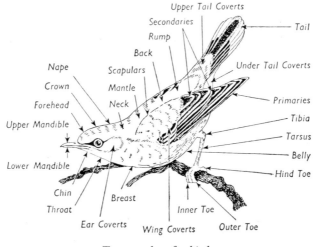

Topography of a bird.

Hide specially built for photographing rooks.

GREY PLOVER

KESTREL

LAPWING

BLACK-HEADED GULL

BLACKBIRD

PEREGRINE

REDSHANK

PARTRIDGE

FULMAR

CURLEW

Some common British birds in

a camera, with which to take shots of such general subjects as habitats and nesting colonies; but if you decide to go further than this and take close-ups of individual birds, then you enter the specialized realm of the bird-photographer, which lies outside the scope of this chapter. There is, however, one item of the bird-photographer's equipment which might be used to great advantage by the field naturalist much more commonly than it is. This is the "hide" within which the photographer conceals himself and his camera at a distance of only a few feet from his subject. Most birds are indifferent to the presence of a hide if it is moved closer in stages, and very few can be watched so closely without it. Consisting of a roll of drab-coloured material—sacking will do—stretched over framework, it is easy to construct oneself.

Birds are much shyer of movement than of

characteristic attitudes of flight.

noise. Indeed, one of the difficulties of the photographer within his hide is, often, to induce his subject to show some sign of life, no matter how much he shouts and whistles! Similarly, when you are watching birds in the field, it is movement rather than noise that you must be careful about, if you wish to study your subject closely and at length. It is surprising how much birds dislike leg-movement. There are comparatively few birds that will allow you to approach them closely over open country, whereas with legs hidden behind a low hedge or stone wall one can approach to within a few yards of them, and stop and raise one's glasses (smoothly and slowly) and study them at one's leisure. With all one's body exposed it is the unrhythmical movements of starting and stopping at which almost every species of bird takes flight.

There is no doubt that birds learn to

*Puffins, showing their distinctive bills which are brightly striped blue, yellow, **and** scarlet.*

differentiate between familiar and unfamiliar objects and harmless and dangerous objects. No one enjoys a closer view of birds than the ploughman and the fisherman. Go down with your binoculars on to the mudflats and see if you can approach the gulls and wading-birds as closely as that stooping figure in dark blue or black gathering mussels or cockles. The importance of dressing inconspicuously has been over-exaggerated, but certainly the more you become a part of a bird's natural and familiar background the more easily it will accept you as a not very suspicious object.

That is one of the charms of studying some nesting sea-birds, such as puffins, which may be so devoid of fear that they will allow you to sit among them and almost touch them; so that, unhampered by the very narrow field of vision permitted by the peep-hole in a hide,

you can observe all their activities at close range hour after hour and day after day, provided that you move gently among them and make no sudden movements. Such an experience is the naturalist's supreme reward in Great Britain, whose birds and beasts have learnt to distrust man. But you will seldom enjoy such rewards in the company of fellow naturalists. A solitary bird-watcher can take liberties with birds that two can never take, and of course the presence of a companion completely destroys your concentration. You cannot pick up a strange call-note with one ear and listen to your companion's conversation with the other; and both eye and ear will miss many things.

On the other hand, if, as a beginner, you can persuade an accomplished naturalist to accompany you on some of your rambles, you will learn more in a single day in the field than from weeks of studying books. It is often difficult to recognize from the most efficiently coloured plates and accompanying text description, birds seen in the field; whereas one does not readily forget the characteristics of a bird seen and correctly identified out of doors; nor, if you are blessed with a good ear, its song or call-note. Once past this stage, however, you will have to decide whether you wish to be a solitary or gregarious bird-watcher; though you can, of course, be the former one day and the latter the next! If you decide on the latter there are many aspects of bird-watching you can enjoy in the company of others, such as taking censuses of the birds of varying habitats at all times of the year and not solely during the nesting season, or "ringing" at an observatory or breeding station.

On your own, of course, there are no limits to your field of activity. Even if you decide to watch birds purely for your own pleasure, without sharing your experiences in notes contributed to some ornithological journal or at some later stage in the form of a paper or book, you will probably find yourself automatically keeping a diary of your observations; so perhaps it is worth noting here that, unless you have a phenomenally retentive memory, any notes you want to record should be jotted down on the spot—though you can, of course, enlarge on them at the end of the day. Indeed, so swiftly changing and complicated are the details of such aspects of bird behaviour as courtship or life among nesting sea-birds, that it is impossible to record notes at the time on all the details without missing some incidents.

And here it may be said that watching birds seriously cannot always be done under pleasant and congenial conditions. In Great Britain, particularly, one has so often to contend with rain, strong winds, and low temperatures. Birds enjoy a moderate rainfall and go about their business normally in wet weather; but it is difficult to use glasses and almost impossible to take notes under such conditions. Wind has the further disadvan-

tage of almost deafening you; moreover, most birds dislike it intensely and remain in shelter. Unless you live on the coast you are more or less wasting your time stirring abroad in a gale. On the coast, however, interesting movements of sea-birds are to be observed under such conditions, and many a storm-battered diving-bird is driven ashore. A cold, calm day is ideal for bird-watching, so far as the birds themselves are concerned; for a snap of frost stimulates them to song and other activities, while a prolonged hard spell results in all sorts of birds turning up in unexpected places; but it can prove a very numbing ordeal for the bird-watcher.

Nevertheless, it is perhaps the endless variety of the ever-changing seasons, and also that of the natural background, that comes to be as strong a lure to the bird-watcher as the birds themselves. The pursuit of birds takes one out into wild and beautiful places in all weathers and at unfamiliar hours when one would not normally think of being abroad. Such experiences are of the salt of life.

Peregrine falcon at eyrie, a raven's old nest.

The habitats of British birds

THE kind of place where a particular bird lives is known as its "habitat." A knowledge of their usual environments is therefore of great importance when learning to recognize birds. Many birds have more than one type of breeding habitat; many more have different ones at different seasons, or when they are on migration.

Closely related birds, too, have quite different preferences in this matter; the three British breeding pipits are good examples. The meadow-pipit is typically found on treeless heaths, moorlands, and waste places; the rock-pipit is more or less confined to rocky coasts and islands, while the tree-pipit is associated with woodlands, bracken banks, and bushy country.

The tree-pipit also provides an example of the value of habitat studies to the experienced ornithologist, absorbed in the central enigma of his hobby: the mind of the bird. There are two apparently similar areas of rough ground: on one several pairs of tree-pipits are nesting, on the other none. The only observable difference between them is that a line of pylons crosses the first area. But these furnish perches whence the male pipits can launch themselves on repeated song-flights over their chosen territories.

The pylons do not affect the available cover or food-supply, two factors which usually influence habitat-selection, but they supply what can only be called a psychological need in the bird's life—the need for a song-perch. This particular need can be fairly easily recognized, but it is quite possible that other more obscure requirements underlie choices of environment which still seem inexplicable to the human observer.

Where "habitat" is mentioned without qualification, the place frequented for nesting is generally meant, and some writers have suggested that where a bird breeds is its ancestral home, so to speak, which various circumstances have forced it to leave at other seasons. In this chapter there will be space to deal only with the breeding habitats of British birds, though a few references to those used in winter or on passage will be made.

Britain is, of course, most deficient in really natural environments for wild-life. The Americans can show vast areas in which man's influence is still confined to small pockets, but in the British Isles it extends to all except the highest mountain-tops and the wildest coasts and islets.

A present-day survey of the principal bird habitats of Britain can conveniently be made by starting from that most affected by man—the completely built-up area—and working, as it were, outwards to those remnants of natural conditions which still remain.

London has the greatest area of continuous building and, in its centre, the breeding bird-life is reduced to a minimum of two species—the house-sparrow and escaped or "London pigeon"—though not of numbers, for there are many thousands of both.

The sparrow, however, has decreased with the disappearance of the horse from the streets and may have shifted slightly from the heart of London to the more open suburbs,

A pair of jays.

Male golden oriole with female on nest in a maple tree.

Pair of goldfinches perching on teasels.

Chaffinches, cock (left) *and hen, on a branch of flowering crab.*

but the pigeon still raises a living, partly with direct human help, and breeds in the cliff-dwellings, just as its wild ancestors, the rock-doves, breed on the sea-cliffs and in the caves of north-west Scotland and Ireland. And when occasional peregrine falcons, raiders normally associated with the wildest country, visit London, they prey on the pigeons and become for a time more urbanized than the sparrows themselves.

As soon as open spaces interrupt the wholly built-up area a number of other species appear. Jackdaws, starlings, house-martins, and swifts are found breeding in the centre of many cities. To these the black redstart, a colonist from the Continent, is adding itself, spreading north and west from the coasts of Kent and Sussex through London to several midland and western cities. It is notable that the first four still nest on cliffs elsewhere in Britain: adaptation from the natural to an artificial habitat has been taking place with the urbanization of the country.

The built-up area is the winter feeding ground of gulls, particularly of the black-headed gull, and the roosting habitat of starlings. Roosting in buildings is a recent development, but is now characteristic of several large British cities.

Squares, parks, gardens, and cemeteries provide the first relief to the cliff-streets and bring with them a range of breeding species which are found throughout the regions characterized by tree and shrub growth.

In a well-known Edinburgh square nine species—greenfinch, chaffinch, house-sparrow, spotted flycatcher, mistle-thrush, song-thrush, blackbird, hedge-sparrow, and tawny owl, with blue tits in a neighbouring garden—breed or have bred in recent years. Carrion-crows nest in London squares and wood-pigeons are now closely associated with the London plane trees. Their seventy-year-old colonization has been accompanied by a change from wariness to confidence in their reaction to man.

The list of birds which have nested exceptionally in city parks could be extended, but the moorhen, where there are ponds, can be included as a regular. In winter, pied wagtails, common and black-headed gulls are daytime inhabitants of parks, especially where these are used as football pitches; churning by energetic athletes acts as a sort of cultivation, which brings worms within reach of the birds.

As the parks and gardens become suburban rather than urban, the number of species increases greatly. The first rookeries appear and the magpie is often more numerous in the no-man's-land round the towns than in the country where the game-preserver's law still runs. The goldfinch is becoming more and more a bird of man's gardens, orchards, and avenues—particularly of horse-chestnuts—thus forgetting a past in which it was the prize of the bird-catcher. The great tit (slightly less urban than the blue tit), robin and wren are also birds of this zone, but unless there are very large oases provided by private grounds, the smaller summer visitors, the warblers, are mainly seen on passage in suburbia. Of larger birds, green and great

Kestrel at former nest of peregrine and raven (see page 23).

25

Black-winged stilts, birds which have bred only once in Britain—in 1945.

spotted woodpeckers, tawny owl and kestrel (in church towers and buildings) may be mentioned here.

Suburbia shades gradually into the farm-land of Britain, but there are four special environments, the result of man's urban-industrial activity which must be considered first.

There is the habitat of industrial ruins and waste places. In some areas, for example South Wales, there is much of this, from the birdless "deserts" near Swansea to the well-covered coal-tips, old quarries and disused collieries of the eastern valleys. Besides the birds of the built-up areas, you may see pied wagtail, grey wagtail, common redstart, swallow, little owl, kestrel, and, more rarely and surprisingly, raven and peregrine falcon. A variety of this type of habitat, the gravel-pits of the London area have recently become the chosen haunt of the little ringed plover, newest of the regular British breeding species.

Ports are more famous for exotic plants and insects that may flourish for a time when introduced with foreign cargoes than for their birds, but in winter they are great centres for herring-gulls, while in summer non-breeding lesser black-backed gulls are to be seen, with cormorants and other sea-birds as occasional visitors. Mallards are often to be seen swimming on the waters of London's docks.

Reservoirs and sewage farms are the Meccas of the urban bird-watcher, for to them on migration or in winter come an amazing variety of water-birds. City reservoirs seldom provide suitable nesting cover, but sewage farms do, and that at Nottingham has become famous for the nesting there in 1945 of the black-winged stilt. But large sewage farms are really human approximations to freshwater marshes, just as reservoirs are to lakes. These are two natural environments which will be dealt with later.

There are several subdivisions of the farm-

Raven, largest member of the crow family, with its young clamouring for food.

Gannet colony on Grassholm, Pembrokeshire, where in 1939 almost six thousand pairs bred.

Gannet, largest British sea-bird, showing its six-foot wing-spread.

land habitat. The birds which breed on cultivated fields anywhere in Britain are remarkably few; sky-lark and lapwing are by far the commonest, but corn-bunting, yellow wagtail, curlew, stone-curlew, oyster-catcher, corn-crake, partridge, red-legged partridge, and quail may occur in different crops and different regions, for some of these are very local or scarce species. The hardly won fields of northern Scotland account for some others; in the Outer Hebrides twites nest under furrows and ringed plovers amid rows of potato plants.

The yellow-hammer, a typical bird of farmland, not only in Britain but throughout Europe, breeds in banks and hedgerows, and brings us to what is perhaps the most important nesting habitat for birds in Britain, the thousands of miles of hedges, mainly of hawthorn, which line the fields from Caithness to Cornwall.

It is the hedges of Britain which make the chaffinch, according to most estimates, the most abundant land-bird. On farm-land investigated in South Wales it was by far the most numerous breeding species, followed by blackbird, hedge-sparrow, and whitethroat, all predominantly hedgerow nesters.

The British hedgerow appears in many forms. It may grow on top of a grass dyke or a low stone wall. It may be doubled along either side of a lane, often with deep, shaded banks. It may develop extraneous bulges, bramble bushes and blackthorn clumps, or be lined with tall elms or ancient, hollow oaks. Again it may be overhung by trailing plants, or be sparse and austere: pure, well-tended hawthorn. The hawthorns may be replaced or supplemented at higher elevations by hazels, or on particular soils by holly, elder, field maple, bird-cherry, dogwood, and many other shrubs; the hedge-base flora may be rich and varied, or dominated by bracken, or almost absent in heavily grazed areas, and all these variations are reflected by changes in the numbers and range of bird species associated with them.

Botanically the hedgerow is an extension, immensely attenuated, of the woodland, and hence some woodland or scrubland birds are hedge-nesters. To list all the birds which may nest in hedges would be a considerable task, but two species can be cited as highly typical of the well-developed hedgerows of southern Britain: the cirl bunting, associated with elm-tree song-perches, and the lesser whitethroat, which is characteristic of lanes that were once drove-roads, with their bushy, straggling hedges.

Small copses are the foci from which the hedges radiate. Bird population studies have shown that the "edge" between two habitats is the home of a dense breeding population; the irregular spinneys of British farmland often have a relatively long edge, combining the advantages of hedgerow cover, the protection of tall trees, and marginal corners of scrub. Over fifty species may nest in such small woods. The total includes the true woodland community, the "common or garden" species noticed in suburbia, and several birds particularly associated with the habitat, such as the chiffchaff, blackcap, and garden-warbler, nesting in low bramble tangle, the nightingale, especially in the hazel copses of southern England, and the pheasant.

The copse is the typical site for a rookery,

for the rook is a bird of agricultural land, seldom found in the big woods. The rooks use their home like the inhabitants of a medieval walled town, issuing from it and bringing back the produce of the fields, either to man's detriment (corn) or advantage (wire-worms), often accompanied by jackdaws chuckling beside them. In well-watered country, spinneys are the sites of heronries, not unusually in company with rookeries. Where the trees are old, remarkable "tenements," housing several species, may develop. In such old trees, but more typically in parkland timber, is found the stock-dove, the wood-pigeon's hole-nesting relative.

The other focus of farmland is the farmhouse and buildings, where an aggregation of minor habitats may combine to make a very important centre of bird-life. Garden and shelter-belt repeat many of the species of hedge and spinney, the buildings attract the group associated with built-up areas and also the barn-owl, while in the orchard, especially if it is old and decayed, a new community is encountered.

The swallow is the typical bird of the farm; it is of great interest, as the one British species

Hen capercaillie, predominantly a bird of Scottish conifer plantations.

Sand-martin and young at their nesting-hole, usually found in river-banks and sand-pits.

completely adapted to man-made nesting sites; only exceptionally in these islands do swallows still breed in caves or hollow trees. Yet it is not an urban bird—investigation has shown that it tends to avoid towns. If the buildings are extensive several pairs may occupy a farm, and they sometimes approach the colonial habits of the house-martins, two or three pairs using the rafters of the same barn.

Orchards are mainly found in the southern half of Britain; in Kent and elsewhere where they are in good order, hawfinch, goldfinch, and the rare and decreasing wryneck are characteristic birds, but in the west, where the cider orchards have decayed with the decline in cider-drinking, the chief inhabitants are hole-nesting species, especially tree-sparrows, tits, green and lesser spotted woodpeckers, and little owls. Mistle-thrushes are fond of orchard sites everywhere, and the quiet which this type of land-use often enjoys

encourages other birds which do not nest in trees at all.

Shading off from cultivated farmland is a vast acreage of rough pasture, found in every British county, but much more extensive in the north and west, where it in turn merges into the moorland. The copses lead in another direction, to the deciduous woodland, which was the principal vegetation of southern Britain when the Romans landed. The birds of oakwood—for the oak was the dominant tree of these ancient forests—are therefore a community of first importance; perhaps they can best be studied today in the Forest of Dean, which contains the largest surviving areas of oak.

Here breed carrion-crow, jay, hawfinch, bullfinch, chaffinch, tree-pipit, tree-creeper, nuthatch, great tit, blue tit, coal-tit, marsh-tit, long-tailed tit, spotted flycatcher, pied flycatcher, goldcrest, willow-warbler, wood-warbler, garden-warbler, blackcap, song-

31

thrush, blackbird, redstart, robin, wren, green, great spotted and lesser spotted woodpeckers, tawny owl, sparrow-hawk, woodpigeon, and woodcock. A number of these, however, are associated with the edges of rides, with gaps and clearings in which thick undergrowth has arisen, or with isolated pine trees that have planted amongst the oaks from time to time. But even if it is not yet possible to subdivide the community with absolute accuracy, the list may safely be said to contain those species which are most truly the inhabitants of oak "high forest" in Britain.

One or two members of the group require special mention; the goldcrest, like the coal-tit, is generally regarded as a conifer bird, with a particular attachment for churchyard yew-trees, but in deciduous woods it nests in the ivy on the trunks of the trees, probably a site adopted when Britain's conifers disappeared. The pied flycatcher has enormously increased in parts of the Forest of Dean since nestboxes were put up, but there is good evidence that it was present in small numbers before that, and it is now found in many woods where there have never been boxes; old woodpecker holes appear to be its favourite "natural" choice. Blackbird and robin may be found nesting in forest sites, steep banks, or under clumps of dead bracken. Sunk in the soft mould, a blackbird's nest is a very different thing from the bulky structure of hedgerow and shrubbery and easily escapes notice unless the bird flies off.

East of the Forest of Dean there are scattered woods of common oak all over England. Their bird population, though normally lacking the pied flycatcher, and often the redstart and wood-warbler, is much the same as that already listed. Westward and northward are woods of the durmast oak, the scrubby oak of Britain's Celtic fringe—a series stretching from Devonshire to Inverness-shire. The pattern of bird-life thins out as we go north; jay, nuthatch, pied flycatcher, blackcap, garden-warbler, green and lesser spotted woodpeckers are eliminated by the time the

Scottish Highlands are reached; the carrion-crow is replaced by the hooded crow, the marsh-tit disappears but the willow-tit remains. It is not a real oakwood bird, but has been discovered in birchwood in Ross-shire.

There is one impressive addition all down the fringe; the buzzard, which is now moving eastward and has reached the Dean. The raven nests in Welsh oakwoods, which are also the home of the last remnant of British kites.

There are other types of deciduous wood in these islands dominated by beech (on chalk), by ash (on limestone), by birch (acid soils), or by alders (wet valleys). Most of them are inhabited by a modification of the oakwood bird community. In pure beech woods, devoid of undergrowth, this is reduced to hole-nesting species, wood-warblers and wood-pigeons. The alders in winter are the haunt of the small finches, goldfinch, lesser redpoll and siskin, often accompanied by blue tits. The birch woods are of interest as the hardiest woodland type in Britain; in them a more northerly bird-life has its southern limit, for in Sutherland, while the ubiquitous chaffinch and willow-warbler are still the commonest species, redwings are heard too regularly in spring to be merely laggard winter visitors, and several nests have been found. Hopes are also entertained that a thorough search of these remote sites might add the brambling to the list of British breeding birds; so far there has been only one certain record. Where the birches meet the moor is found the black grouse, a species which has been seriously reduced in recent years.

But between the oakwoods and the northern birchwoods lie the remains of native conifer forest; the ancient woods of Scots pine, now principally located in the Spey Valley, with outliers north and west.

Four birds are inevitably associated by ornithologists with these woods, for this is their undoubted stronghold in Britain today, where two of them, crossbill and crested tit, have developed local races confined to the

Pair of crossbills; hen feeding young with grubs.

Pair of reed-buntings.

Linnets.

Greenfinches and young.

Yellow-hammers.

neighbourhood. Another, the siskin is spreading and has nested in many Scottish and occasionally in English and Welsh counties. The fourth, the capercaillie, died out as the pines were felled, but was re-introduced and profited by the private planting of conifers to re-colonize much of central Scotland.

With this quartet many of the oakwood birds are associated; in fact, some, like the tree-creeper and coal-tit, are conifer birds that have adapted themselves, as the capercaillie could not, to deciduous woods. Chaffinch, bullfinch, goldcrest, great spotted woodpecker, long-eared owl and sparrow-hawk are other characteristic species of conifer woods.

But the area of native Scots pine is very small compared with the acreages of introduced species—pines, spruces, Douglas firs, and larches—which have been planted throughout Britain in the past two hundred years. Many plantations were felled in the two wars, but today there are more young plantations, mainly the property of the Forestry Commission, than ever before in living memory, and the effect of afforestation on bird-life is more and more engaging the attention of bird-watchers.

Generally speaking, the planted conifers of Britain, as they attain tree height, are colonized by a sparse population from the deciduous woods, principally the small group of species listed above, but lacking the Strathspey rarities. The Continental race of the common crossbill, however, has been established for many years now in East Anglia, and periodically invades other districts. But it normally nests in scattered trees or the pine hedges which are a feature of the Norfolk brecks, and not in closed woods at all.

Whether other denizens of the European forests, such as the goshawk, which nested in Britain formerly, will reach the woods when they are mature, no one can say; at present the focus of interest is on what happens in the early stages of establishment.

When a bare hillside is fenced in and protected from grazing animals, there is a rapid growth of plants with which the young trees have to contend. This growth is favourable cover for such birds as grasshopper-warbler, whinchat, and stonechat, whereas the species of open ground are gradually eliminated. If afforestation is accompanied by a vole-plague, there may also be local abundance of the short-eared owl. As the trees grow up, the inevitable willow-warbler becomes dominant, in a habitat suitable also for the rare Montagu's harrier, and recent increases of this bird in some districts are believed to be due to the large areas of young plantings. Black grouse also profit by this stage, but they feed on the tree shoots and are not welcomed by foresters; woodcock are not uncommon, and will persist in the closed canopy, when all the original and intermediate inhabitants of the area have disappeared.

Such is a brief outline of some of the changes which take place, and on which very much more detailed work in all parts of Britain remains to be done.

Between the woodlands and the open habitats are the scrubby commons or dry heaths. The character of the bird population will vary considerably according to the amount and nature of the cover, but in southern England if hawthorns are present—and they almost certainly will be—this is the habitat of red-backed shrike and turtle-dove. Most of the other species which occur have already been noticed, but if the common is a gorse-clad heath in southern England, a community containing that great rarity the Dartford warbler may be found; while, if clumps of pine are added, conditions are favourable for the hobby, scarcest of British falcons. But the normal inhabitants of gorse-heath are linnets, yellow-hammers, whitethroats, stonechats, blackbirds, and hedge-sparrows, attractive to the parasitic cuckoo; many hours, however, can be spent searching and observing this type of country for very little result.

As the heath gets barer, its bird-life changes, until it approaches that of open downland or breckland. These former homes of the great bustard are now inhabited by its nearest relative surviving in Britain, the stone-curlew. Associated with this fascinating species, one of the most eagerly sought after by bird-photographers, are sky-lark, wood-lark, wheatear (nesting in rabbit-holes), nightjar and lapwing; in the brecks the ringed plover also occurs, miles from the coast. Bracken and isolated bushes may increase the number of species, but in a short chapter only typical communities of each habitat can be dealt with.

Heaths, downs, and brecks belong on the whole to the dry south and east; in the north and west they are replaced by grass moors, bracken, and heather moors, and over millions of acres ruled by these vegetation types the meadow-pipit, chief fosterer of the cuckoo, is the dominant species. Where the moorland is at its most barren, as on the Pennant sandstone ridges of South Wales, the pipit is accompanied only by occasional pairs of sky-larks, by wheatears if the rock outcrops, and by scattered colonies of lapwings, but where an acid flora is well developed and pools or patches of cotton-grass bog are found, the population is increased in variety and for the first time the numerical superiority of the passerine or song-birds, which has obtained over all the many environments so far described, is challenged.

The species of this sort of moorland, anywhere from Breconshire northward, may be sky-lark, meadow-pipit, merlin, short-eared owl, curlew, snipe, dunlin, golden plover, lapwing, and red grouse, with mallard, teal, or a colony of black-headed gulls if there is open water in the vicinity; only the first two of these are perching birds, known as passerines, though north of Wales the twite may be added to the community. In Scotland boggy moors are favourite sites for gull colonies, especially of the common gull, while in the extreme north such rarities as hen-harrier, whimbrel, greenshank, and great and Arctic skuas are moorland nesters, providing a link with the Arctic tundra where countless thousands of birds, chiefly waders, rear their broods in the short summer.

To find Arctic-Alpine conditions in Britain, however, the moorland must be followed not only northward but upward to the three-thousand-foot contour in the Scottish Highlands. Here, only a few miles from the Caledonian pine forest of Strathspey, is another relict community living in conditions unaffected by man; in descending order of abundance, ptarmigan, dotterel, and snow-bunting are its members.

Inset in the moorlands and playing rather the rôle of copses in agricultural land are gorges and inland cliffs, often the stronghold of a rich population of birds of prey. Here in different regions may nest ravens, carrion- or hooded crows, kestrels, peregrines, buzzards, and the golden eagle, together with ring-ouzels, wheatears (on the screes), and wrens. If bushes and long heather grow amongst the rocks, a whole association of small birds appears even up to the two-thousand-foot contour, and the banshee shrieking of a disturbed peregrine falcon may be succeeded by the trilling song of the wood-warbler, which we last met in a lowland beechwood.

From the moorlands flow innumerable streams, brooks, or burns, but almost throughout Britain they are frequented in spring by four species of birds: grey wagtail, ring-ouzel, dipper, and common sandpiper. All may be seen elsewhere, but together they form the community of fast-flowing water. As the pace of the current abates and sandy banks appear, sand-martin and kingfisher are found, and the ring-ouzel, which is tied to the moorland, disappears. When backwaters occur and blocks of drift accumulate, the moorhen is added, while on shingle-beds in Scotland the oyster-catcher and ringed plover nest. Mallard may breed and herons fish all down its course, but they will be more numerous in the lower reaches, where in slow-flowing stretches, half hidden by aquatic vegetation, little grebe and coot are found.

The broad river is a great highway of bird-life, and many birds rest or feed by it that are not truly of the type that live by rivers.

Buzzards at the nest; once common, they now nest only in hill districts of Britain.

Red-necked phalarope by the nest.

Most of the breeding species of duck, for example, are seen on rivers in winter, but really prefer lakes or pools in the nesting season; the one exception is perhaps the goosander, whose southern breeding limit at present is in Northumberland.

Freshwater lakes and marsh can be taken together as one major habitat, since the marsh often consists of a series of zones round a centre of open water. Standing in the water may be beds of reeds, water-lilies, bog-bean, mare's tails, club-rushes or water bistort; these may be succeeded by a wet zone in which reeds and sedges meet, to be followed by a dry sedge zone, or by a zone of Molinia grass tussocks, bog myrtle, and lank heather, or by rushes and iris clumps; finally there may be sallow copses, or alder swamp, or rushy pasture or deer-grass moor.

These are only examples of the many possible permutations according to acidity, alti-tude, and latitude, but certain members of the bird community remain remarkably constant: reed-bunting, sedge-warbler, little grebe, moorhen, and coot nest by the shallow lochans of North Uist and by ponds within a few miles of London. In Finland, however, three types of lake, suited to divers, to grebes, and to diving ducks, have been distinguished, and these can be recognized even in the humanized British Isles. The black-throated and red-throated divers nest by lochans in the Scottish hills and islands—though they have slightly different preferences; the great crested, black-necked, and Slavonian grebes usually require floating vegetation or reedy cover, while in the case of tufted duck and pochard a fringe of sedge tussocks or rushes is the choice of environment.

Other birds are associated with these three lake-types; by the diver-lochs of the north are found colonies of gulls, and ducks such as mallard, wigeon, and the very rare scoter, while on their heathery or rushy islets—always magnetic to waterfowl—the greylag-goose still nests. Near this type are the bog-bean and cotton-grass bogs where the red-necked phalarope holds out. In southern Britain the reed-beds of the grebe-lake attract the semi-domesticated mute swan and at the other end of the scale the reed-warbler. But the very similar and rarer marsh-warbler has a distinct habitat in drier reed and nettle-beds shadowed by osiers. The verges of the diving duck-lake are suitable for the grasshopper-warbler, for the water-rail, for the introduced Canada goose and for those surface-feeding ducks not yet mentioned: gadwall, garganey, pintail, shoveler, which also nest in water-meadows and bogs at a distance from the water; here they are joined by waders such as curlew, snipe, and redshank. The rarity of southern bogland is the spotted crake, which very few naturalists have ever set eyes on in the breeding season.

The marshes and fens of East Anglia were the haunts of species that have now vanished, though one, the avocet, has just made a remarkable "come-back," and two more, black-tailed godwit and black tern, breed occasionally; but in the reed-beds of the Norfolk Broads and their neighbourhood another relict community survives: bearded tit, marsh-harrier, and bittern.

The sallows and osiers surrounding many lakes and marshes are a favourite nesting place of the lesser redpoll, and often attract species with less specialized requirements: carrion-crows, wood-pigeons, wrens, and other small birds.

The fresh water enters the sea in estuaries where thousands of birds gather on passage and in winter; breeding species, however, may be few and it is not until the coastline is reached that new habitats become clearly defined.

The low shore with salt-marshes is closely related to the freshwater marsh; where there is dry ground and some cover an interesting community may develop. Such a strand a few miles east of Edinburgh has retained a population constant in character over at least twenty years and consisting of sky-lark, eider duck, dunlin, redshank, ringed plover,

lapwing, and common tern. A few yards inland, the marsh birds appear: reed-bunting, sedge-warbler, snipe, and moorhen; while a little farther along the coast the sand-dunes begin, with an almost complete change of species: linnet, meadow-pipit, wheatear, sheld-duck, stock-dove (the last three nesting in rabbit-holes) with lesser tern on the shingle where common tern and ringed plover carry over from the salt-marsh. Another half-mile and the rock outcrops on the shore; here rock-pipits chirp and purple sandpipers and turnstones can be seen congregating in winter. Thus in about one square mile four distinct environments show their distinctive birds.

The oyster-catcher is absent from the Forth as a breeding species, and virtually so between Norfolk and Dorset, but along most of the British coastline, shingle, sand or low rock, it is the characteristic, obvious bird. In the bird sanctuaries of north Norfolk it is found with redshank and ringed plover nesting close to the great terneries, where common, Sandwich, lesser, and occasional pairs of Arctic

Black-throated diver, which nests in northern Scotland.

and roseate terns breed. Although large colonies of black-headed gulls are sited on dunes, and common gulls, herring-gulls, and kittiwakes have all been recorded nesting on such shores, terns are the typical sea-birds of the dunes and low islands.

Low rocky coasts with numerous islets are probably most developed along the sea-lochs of the West Highlands. This, above all, is the home of the red-breasted merganser, the black guillemot on loose boulders and debris, the Arctic tern on the skerries and the eider amongst long heather or on short sea turf.

As the cliffs rise in height, a new group appears—cormorant, shag, gannet, kittiwake, guillemot and razorbill. Along the cliff-top in crevices and burrows are Manx shearwaters, storm-petrels, Leach's petrels (in four remote Hebridean stations), and puffins, the first and last especially victimized by the great black-backed gulls, which, with the lesser black-backs and herring-gulls, build their open nests in the same zone.

It is hard to place the fulmar petrel, for in its great expansion from the rocks of St. Kilda it has used cliffs, steep banks, ruins,

Choughs, photographed by flashlight, in a disused North Wales lead-mine.

Black-headed gull about to land on its nest in a tuft of rushes.

sand-dunes, and even inland outcrops as nesting sites. Land-birds also inhabit the sea-cliffs; indeed, their sanctuary may have saved raven and buzzard in the days of great persecution, though they could not save the sea-eagle. The cliff-nesting of jackdaw, starling, house-martin, and swift has already been mentioned. Two other birds are characteristic: the rock-dove and the chough: except in

North Wales, this rarest member of the crow family is now confined to the sea-coast.

Here is the richest, most impressive, least accessible bird habitat in Britain, of whose teeming life only a glimpse has been possible; but it makes a fitting conclusion to this survey, which began in Central London and has covered the environments in which our 186 regular breeding bird species nest.

British birds described

The classified list of British birds compiled by H. F. Witherby is now accepted as standard by leading ornithologists. It has been followed in the preparation of this book. In this chapter, which naturally constitutes a major part of the book, each section deals with a family or group of birds. The reader seeking reference to an individual bird but uncertain of its family will find the index the simplest and quickest guide to the information sought.

CROWS, STARLINGS, AND THE ORIOLE

CROWS and starlings are to be found in every corner of Britain, from the heart of the industrial towns to the wildest sea-cliffs and mountain crags. Most of them are large, black birds, and the common rook (18 in. from tip of beak to tip of tail) will serve as a stock example. Its grey beak, bald forehead, and baggy "plus-fours," together with its rolling gait, distinguish it from the

Hooded crow, common resident of Scotland.

carrion-crow (18–19 in.), which is sable-black from beak to featherless legs, with which it more commonly hops than walks. Young rooks, however, lack the characteristic bare face, and one must look for their "plus-fours" and, on a sunny day, for their purple sheen—green on the carrion's plumage. Moreover, rooks are usually seen in flocks of hundreds: whereas crows are commonly in pairs and seldom more than a dozen or twenty together; nor is there any difficulty in distinguishing the crow's harsh *kraa-aa* from the rook's familiar caw and many other call-notes.

Rooks occur in all parts of the British Isles except Shetland, and numbers of Continental rooks, together with crows and jackdaws, also winter in Britain; but the carrion crow is mainly replaced in the Scottish Highlands and the Isle of Man by the hooded crow (18–19 in.), which has a grey back and underparts. Where the two species overlap interbreeding may occur, the resulting offspring being difficult to identify. In England the "hoodie" is mainly a winter visitor only to the more easterly counties.

In the west of Britain, from Cornwall northward, and in the Scottish Highlands, ravens (25 in.) are to be found in rook and crow country. Although very much larger than either rooks or crows, notably so of heavy, shaggy head and powerful bill, the raven is another all-black crow and could be mistaken for one in distant flight. However, points to remember about the raven, apart from its size, are that its wings are long and straight; that it flies direct and fast and usually at a considerable height, often soars, and has a trick of intermittently rolling over on to its back, with wings half-closed; that it often flies alone and seldom in greater force than

Sky-lark and brood of young in a patch of ground-ivy.

Pair of meadow-pipits.

Adult pied wagtails and one young bird, distinguishable by its yellow face

Pair of yellow wagtails: the male is on the right.

Pair of grey wagtails in winter plumage.

Tree-creepers and young at their nest.

a family of four or five together; and that it is a noisy bird, constantly uttering its unmistakable croaking *prook-prook*.

Here and there on west-coast cliffs one may be fortunate enough to see a pair or a small flock of the now rare choughs (15 in.), and know them by their purple-black plumage and curved red beaks and red legs. Their clear musical calls are higher pitched than the familiar *tchack* of the jackdaw (13 in.). Though the invariable companion of the rooks in fields in all parts of Britain, the jackdaw is also a bird of the cliffs. Much of a size with the chough, and considerably smaller than the rook, the jackdaw is distinguished by its dark-grey hood and glassy eye.

Very different from any of these crows is the pied magpie (18 in.), with its very long, diamond-shaped tail and its black parts all greens and purples in the sun. When the bird is in the air that long tail and feeble, fluttering flight are unmistakable; while, when skulking in hedgerow or coppice, its harsh chattering betrays it.

Nor would you suspect the exotic-looking jay (13–14 in.) of being a crow, with its claret-coloured plumage set off by blue-and-white wings, white rump, and black tail. Its raucous, squawking voice is, however, similar to that of other crows, and if in spring you hear an extraordinary medley of mewing, crooning, and gurgling, interspersed with falsetto mimicries of other birds' notes, coming from the heart of the woods, this will indicate an assembly of jays.

So much for the crows, and there is no need to describe the starling (8–9 in.) of the chimney-pot, with its shivering wings and shaggy throat, its piercing "cat-calls" and musical mimicries of almost every other bird's song and call-notes. There is no other bird with that spangled, iridescent plumage, though young starlings are a plain dark-brown with whitish throats; none so energetic and noisy; and none which congregate to roost in scores of thousands on buildings and in plantations and reed-beds in and around the largest cities. Many of the starlings in these vast roosts are, however, winter visitors to Britain from Europe.

There is another starling, which occasionally wanders to the east coast of Britain in summer and autumn from its true home in South-east Europe. This is the rose-coloured starling (8–9 in.) which, though it resembles the common starling in flight, is a strikingly plumaged bird at close quarters, its rose-pink body contrasting with black wings, tail, and crested head. The juvenile, however, is very similar to the young starling.

Finally, there is the beautiful golden oriole (9–10 in.), which occasionally nests in southern England, but which is mainly a rare spring visitor from Africa to the eastern and southern coasts. Although the cock is a brilliant sulphur-yellow bird with black wings, many of the visitors to Britain are the brown and bronze-gold immature birds.

In addition to points of plumage, voice, and flight there are other factors which help one to identify British birds. No one could mistake a colony of rooks, for example; not only on account of the noisy cawing they make all day long in spring and summer, but from their habit of building their stick nests, bound together with earth, in the upper branches of tall trees; though in Scotland a stand of comparatively low pine trees is a favourite site.

Jackdaw and young.

41

Pair of rooks: compare these members of the crow family with the bird on the page opposite.

During the nesting season the constant two-way shuttle from rookery to near-by fields is a familiar spectacle: for rooks consume an enormous quantity of grubs harmful to the farmer's crops, taking a fair measure of grain by way of reward for their invaluable services.

The carrion-crow, on the other hand, is a solitary and secretive nester (though a couple of dozen crows may roost in the same wood in the winter), and commonly builds its stout nest of sticks or heather-stems in the fork of a tree, though often in bushes in hilly country and on cliff-ledges on the coast. And, unlike the rook, it is mainly a carrion eater, besides taking heavy toll of the eggs of ground-nesting birds. This is also true of the wary hooded crow, which builds a similar nest in some lone tree in a highland glen or on the extreme point of a rocky headland, besides nesting on the ground on heather-clad northern islands.

The raven, almost exclusively a carrion feeder, is characteristically a bird of the most inaccessible sea-cliffs and mountain crags, building its massive nest of seaweed-stems or of heather-stalks and earth on some un-approachable ledge; but in the south-west of England the nest may be placed in a pine tree at no great height, and tree-nesting ravens were common in many parts of England a hundred years ago.

As the constant flock companion of rooks in the fields, jackdaws might be expected to share their tree colonies; but only occasion-ally are one or two pairs to be found nesting among the rooks in the latter's old nests. Normally the jackdaws establish their own small nesting colonies in ruined castles and abbeys, in woods of lopped trees, or on inland crags or sea-cliffs. If the nesting-hole is a small one, a pair of jackdaws will be satisfied with a mere lining of wool or grass; but if the cavity is large, an attempt will be made to fill it with enormous quantities of sticks—a cart-load being the record of one pair!

On west-coast cliffs the jackdaw meets the

chough (15 in.), which, however, never ventures more than a few yards inland from the cliff-top in search of food, mainly beetles. Whether it wedges its nest into a crack in the cliff or places it on a ledge in a cave, the chough always constructs a proper one of sticks or bracken-stalks with a good lining of wool or hair.

Although the magpie inhabits such widely different terrains as the covert, field, and hedgerow country of the heart of England, or the coombe and down country of the southwest, or the rolling, treeless dales and fells of the north, and also penetrates into the Scottish Highlands, it is conservative in its nesting habits, usually building its nest in a tall tree or in a bush in hill country. It is a bulky structure of stalks with a thorny dome. Like other crows the magpie's diet is omnivorous, including carrion, birds' eggs, grubs, insects, and vegetable matter.

This also applies to the jay, exclusively a woodland bird, not found in hill country. Skulking in the innermost parts of wood or plantation, it seldom ventures out, except on its early morning raids on the peas in adjacent gardens. It does, however, nest in thick scrub in gardens and orchards, building a nest of twigs and earth with a thick lining of black, fibrous roots.

The starling's typical nesting places are holes in buildings and trees, in which it fashions a rough nest of straws and feathers. But during the past two centuries the starling has colonized the remotest islands around Britain. In such outposts there may be no trees or shrubs and few buildings, but stone dykes and even cliffs and boulder-beaches provide these pioneers with all the nesting cover they require. In Shetland, where there has long been established a distinct race of starlings with darker-plumaged young, they may be heard "singing" merrily from chinks in the dykes, and their very harsh notes sound

Carrion-crow, distinguished from the rook by its feathered face.

strange to the southerner's ear. But there, as on the mainland of Britain, young and old band together after the nesting season to quarter the fields industriously in search of the grubs and insects which are their main food.

A rare vagrant to the British Isles is the nutcracker (12–13 in.), which is brown speckled with white, has a long, pointed beak and a white border to its black-brown tail.

FINCHES, BUNTINGS, AND SPARROWS

Identification of finches, sparrows, and buntings is made more difficult by the fact that in most cases the cock bird's plumage differs from that of the hen. But let us make a start with the cock house-sparrow (6 in.), whose grey crown and black bib distinguish his impudent and aggressive lordship from his sober brown mate. If your acquaintance with the sparrow is restricted to the soot-begrimed specimens of large towns, you would be surprised at the clean bright plumage of the country sparrows; for, though very familiar in city street, warehouse, and factory, the sparrow has now, like the starling, established itself on the remotest islands of the Hebrides and even of Shetland. But whether it be under the eaves of the manor house on the Isle of

Tree-sparrow perching, with food.

Lundy, eleven miles from the nearest shore of the Bristol Channel, or in the flower-studded thatch of a Highland crofter's house, a thousand feet up in the hills, the sparrow remains true to its tradition of never nesting away from man's habitation, stuffing its untidy nest of straws into convenient holes in all these varied dwelling-places.

There is, however, another British sparrow, the tree-sparrow (5–6 in.), which prefers to nest in holes in hollow trees. Though widely distributed throughout Britain, and a bird of passage along the east coast, its nesting colonies are extremely localized and it is very much less numerous than the house-sparrow. Should you locate a colony—and the wooded fringe of a marsh or sewage farm is a favourite locality—you will find them immediately recognizable by their copper-coloured crowns and white collars, while their distinctive whistling call-note is higher pitched and more melodious than the house-sparrow's metallic chirrup. Both are grain and insect-feeders, though the tree-sparrow never raids the farmer's cornfields in those enormous flocks common to the house-sparrow, when the latter takes a country holiday in the late summer and joins forces with finches and buntings on the shocks and stubbles.

In these composite flocks, which are sometimes thousands strong, there will be chaffinches, greenfinches, and linnets. If the sparrow is the bird of the town, the gaily coloured chaffinch (6 in.) is the bird of village and farmstead, especially in the Scottish Highlands; and its short bursts of rollicking song and metallic *pink-pink* are to be heard the day long in spring from garden and orchard, woodland copse and highland glen, from end to end of the British Isles. It is one of the three commonest small birds of Britain, and its numbers are increased during the winter by large flocks of immigrants from the Continent.

With its slate-blue head and nape, pink breast, and snowy-white patches on shoulders and wings, the cock chaffinch cannot be mistaken for any other British bird; while the hen, though mainly greenish in colour, is also

44

Hawfinch, which uses its strong beak for splitting fruit-stones.

distinguished by those white shoulder "flashes." Unmistakable, too, is its exquisitely constructed nest of grasses and mosses, with its neat hair-lining and external decoration of lichens, gummed together with spiders' webs. Where, as in the wooded glens of the Highlands, the nest is built in the angle between branch and bole of a birch tree its camouflage of lichens renders it almost invisible. In England, however, the nest may commonly be found in bushes and hedgerows.

Very often the winter flocks of chaffinches include numbers of bramblings (6 in.) from Scandinavian forests, some of which feed in stackyards and beechwoods, while others travel on as far south as the Mediterranean. Resembling the chaffinch in general appearance, bramblings are easily distinguished by their brown or blackish heads and orange-buff breasts, while in flight a white rump catches the eye.

Even more conspicuous than the chaffinches among the mixed flocks on the corn-stubbles are the greenfinches (6 in.), when a compact band of them whirrs up, revealing golden bars on the wings and on the outside edges of their short, cleft tails, vividly bright in the cocks. There is no mistaking these plump olive-green finches either, when you come upon them in the hedgerows, with their stout seed-cracking beaks and heads stained purple with blackberry juice. They are no less distinctive in spring, when the hedgerows in most parts of Britain are pleasantly noisy the day long with their bell-like chirrupings and lazy, sleepy *doowee* and nasal *tswee* call-notes. From time to time the cocks circle out from hedge-top or tree, in a mazy bat-like flight, with twittering songs of chirrups and trills, while the hens, often in small colonies, are sitting on their nests of twigs and moss in the hedge.

Though there is no other English bird resembling the greenfinch, it would be possible in the Highlands to confuse it with the smaller, slimmer, olive-green siskin (5 in.). The latter also has those vivid golden bars on wings and tail-edges, though the cock has a black crown and chin; and it, too, employs that same bat-like song-flight out from some tall conifer, on a high branch of which the hen has built her nest of dead twigs and lichens. You are not likely to find a siskin nesting in England, but during the winter little flocks—some, no doubt, visitors from the Continent—are often to be found in riverside alder and birch trees, swinging all ways up while feeding on their fruits and catkins.

An interesting habit of birds is that of different species flocking together while on migration and during their winter wanderings through the countryside. Thus, seldom indeed do siskins hunt the English riversides alone, but nearly always in the company of lesser redpolls (5 in.), which also nest in similar localities to the siskin in the Highlands, besides sparsely in most of the English counties. The redpolls, however, are much more catholic in their choice of nesting sites, and you may find colonies of their roughly

Greenfinch at its nest in a gorse-bush.

fashioned nests of twigs and grass-stems in such varied sites as hedges and bushes, birch-trees and forest pines, reed-beds and alder swamps, and even in old heather; and be advised of their presence by their insect-like, sibilant, twittering chorus, distinct from the sweet *pee-wee* notes and cascades of song of their siskin companions.

With the redpolls we come to a group of finches providing some difficulty in identification. The lesser redpoll itself, though it has a crimson brow and breast to relieve its streaky-brown mantle and silvery undersides, is by no means easy to distinguish from the siskin in the twilit woods, though its tail is noticeably longer and more forked. Then, in the winter, north Britain is visited by an Arctic-nesting redpoll, the mealy (5 in.). In the field, the expert can usually distinguish the latter from the lesser redpoll by its larger size and paler plumage, which in some cases is almost whitish.

The probability is that you may never see a mealy redpoll, but there still remain two very similarly plumaged finches, the linnet (5 in.) and the twite (5 in.). Generally speaking, linnet and redpoll do not occupy the same districts, for the former is essentially an English bird, and the latter a Scottish one. Where they overlap, particularly during their winter wanderings, one has to bear in mind that the linnet is a larger bird than the redpoll; while in breeding plumage the cock linnet has, in addition to its crimson crown and breast, a chestnut mantle. Moreover, while their call-notes are rather similar, the linnet's sweet, yet metallic, twittering song, sometimes rendered by a choir of hundreds of birds in bush or tree, is unmistakable. To distinguish between the songs of linnet and twite, however, is a matter of experience, for the latter also habitually sing in chorus.

The twite, like the redpoll, is essentially a Scottish bird, but, unlike the latter, a bird of the moorland fringes and seashore hinterland and even cliff-tops. It is much more numerous in the western and northern islands, where it is a typical bird of the crofting town-

Twite, common on the moors of northern Britain, seen at its nest in the heather.

ships, than on the mainland. In the winter, when numbers of twites and linnets reach the shores of Britain from the Continent, you may well find mixed flocks in coastal districts and have difficulty in making out the twites' yellow bills. Their plump bodies, small round heads, and tawny underparts are better clues to their identity.

Both twite and linnet may breed in colonies, though more often singly; but whereas the linnet is characteristically a bird of gorse-common, hedgerow, and garden, the twite's nesting site is typically a stone dyke or heather. Both, being finches, are, of course, grain and insect feeders, while in Shetland the twite has a bad name with the crofters on account of its partiality for cabbage and turnip seedlings.

Sometimes "charms" of goldfinches (5 in.) mingle with the immense flocks of finches on the stubbles; but these, perhaps the most exquisitely coloured of all the small British birds, are typically birds of wasteland (where grow the thistles that are one of their main food sources) of the less wild regions of Britain, and are scarce in Scotland. Reduced by bird-catchers almost to extinction during the late nineteenth century, the "charms" of these little twittering finches, with their strikingly banded black, white, and ruby-red heads and brilliant gold-and-black wings, are today the most prized adornment of every down and "bottom" in southern England and the Home Counties. In the breeding season, when the "charms" break up, the mated pairs move into orchards and gardens, where the hen-bird builds her compact little nest of roots and mosses, into which wool is woven, on a lichenous fruit-tree bough. Her mate twitters, from a high perch in a neighbouring tree, a sprightly song which is higher-pitched than the greenfinch's and ends in a canary-like trill.

To complete this section on finches we have to consider three predominantly woodland species, all distinctively and beautifully plumaged. The first is the heavily built bull-finch (6 in.), unmistakable in its black cap, grey mantle, and gorgeous hunting-pink waistcoat, which is much paler in the hen bird. It is the shy and rather seldom seen inhabitant of orchards and heavily shrubbed woodlands in England, and of birch-woods and juniper-studded pine-forests in the Scot-tish Highlands. When seen, the bullfinch is nearly always in family parties or larger groups, but it is such a secretive bird that the first indication of its presence is usually its whispered, high-pitched, piping note, uttered so softly that, rather than definitely hearing it, one "imagines" it. Only then may one get a fleeting glimpse of its distinctive white rump as it dives into the undergrowth again. Fruit-growers, however, are afforded more evidence of the bullfinch's comparative numerousness than they like, inasmuch as its staple food is the buds and berries of a variety of trees and shrubs. Rarely indeed will you hear its low warbling song near its nest, which is placed in a dense shrubbery of evergreens or a thick hedge (especially of box or yew), or in the heavy undergrowth of a plantation. The nest, however, is unmistakable, being built of thin twigs and moss, with a thick lining of fine black roots, placed only a few feet above the ground.

Another fruit-eating finch, this time of their hard kernels, is the shy and secretive haw-finch (6–7 in.). You may first be apprised of its presence by the thin sound of its "seeping" flight-note, when a flock circles over the woods at some hundreds of feet. With their plump bodies and triangular-shaped wings they much resemble starlings. This may be the only hawfinch note you will ever hear, for they are extraordinarily silent birds, though the cock does have a primitive two-noted song, rather like the bullfinch's, of which the first note is a tinny one and the second a lower crooning note. In winter a favourite retreat of the hawfinch is a hawthorn plantation or mixed wood on the outskirts of a garden-city or even of a large town. Here they band together in flocks a score or two strong, and you will be left in no doubt as to their iden-tity, for no other bird has that enormous square head and pinkish-white or steely-blue stone-crushing beak, or that exotically brilli-ant ruddy-brown plumage and short, square, flame-coloured tail with a white-spotted bor-der. In such habitats, too, as well as in orchards and wooded gardens, the hawfinch builds its unsubstantial nest of roots and lichens on a foundation of twigs, often placing it on a branch of a tree. Though much more numerous than its secretive ways would lead one to suppose, the hawfinch is very local in its distribution throughout most of England and lowland Scotland, and is essentially a midland and southern England species.

The only other finch, which habitually flies at a considerable height above both its winter-ing and nesting woods, with a noisy *peep-peep*, is the crossbill (6–7 in.). Although you can see crossbills nesting in roadside pine trees on the brecklands of Norfolk and Suffolk, the native British crossbill most truly resident in the British Isles is the Scottish one, which is distinguished by a somewhat stouter beak. It is an inhabitant of pine forests and especially larch groves in the north and central Highlands, and its habits are much the same as those of the common crossbill. Let it be said at once that those twisted mandibles, with which the crossbill wrenches out the seeds from larch and pine cones, are not the obvious distinguishing feature one might suppose, for they become apparent only at close range. As the bird normally feeds at a considerable height, swinging upside down like a little parrot, it seldom affords one a close view, except when it flies down to pool or rain-gutter to drink. Nevertheless, the rosy-red cock and yellowish-green hen cannot be mistaken for any other British bird. If you cannot see them, you can still

Great tits.

Blue tits.

Coal-tits.

Marsh-tits.

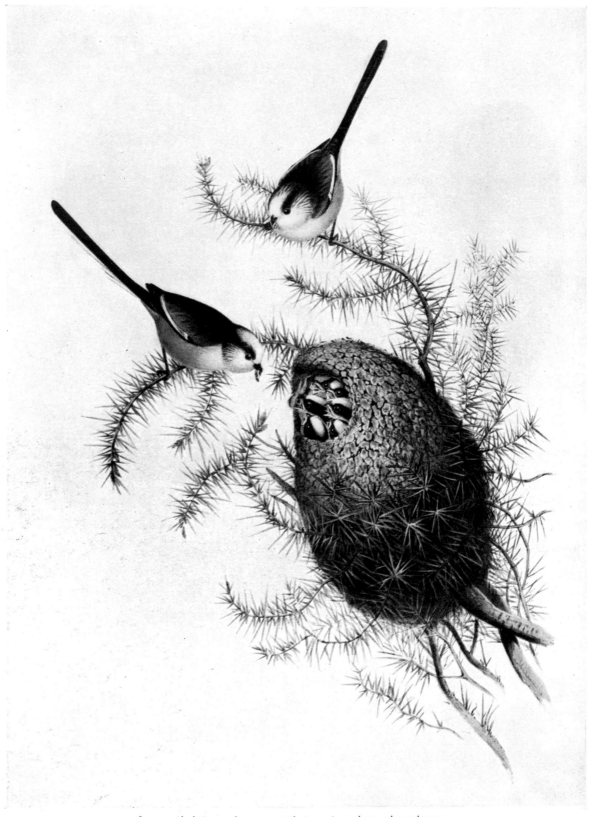

Long-tailed tits and young at their curious dome-shaped nest.

locate them by the continual "plop-plop" of discarded larch cones—its staple food—falling to the ground; by the chirping *tyup-tyup-tyup* of the old birds; by the ceaseless *vee-tu, vee-tu, vee-tu* of the young ones begging food from their parents. A cock will often interrupt its cone-wrenching to circle out from the trees, or to perch on the spring tip of one, and utter its short but brilliant canary-like song. During the nesting season this conspicuous song-flight also reveals the approximate whereabouts of the flattish nest of twigs, grasses, and wool, high up in larch or pine.

So much for the finches. Included in their large flocks on the summer stubbles and about the stackyards in winter will almost certainly be buntings. There will be plump corn-buntings (7 in.), with nothing but their heavy build and low labouring flight, with legs hanging down, to distinguish them: for their plumage is a nondescript streaky drab-brown, with not even the white outer tail-feathers characteristic of other buntings. There will certainly be yellow-hammers (6–7 in.), the cocks' mustard-yellow heads and breasts gleaming in the sun, the duller-plumaged hens distinguished from corn-buntings by their slimmer build, yellow underparts and bright chestnut rumps. There may also be a few reed-buntings (6 in.), the cocks with black heads and white collars, the hens distinguished by buff eye-stripes and dark moustachial streaks.

Near the coast and in the hills these mixed flocks may be augmented in winter by numbers of immigrant snow-buntings (6–7 in.) from northern Europe and Arctic islands. These you will have no difficulty in recognizing by the large amount of white on their wings, tails, and underparts, especially in the cocks.

In southern England, especially in the West Country, there will be cirl-buntings (6 in.). The cocks are easy enough to distinguish with their black throats and olive-green breast-bands; but hen cirl-buntings are difficult to differentiate from hen yellow-hammers,

the only difference being that their rumps are olive-brown instead of chestnut colour.

Finally there is the Lapland bunting (6 in.), which is a rather rare bird of passage on the eastern and southern seaboards of Britain, and of which you are likely to see only one or two in a lifetime, unless you spend a migratory season at one of the coastal observatory stations. Not unlike a large reed-bunting, the cock has a black face and gorget, the hen a copper-coloured nape.

To return to buntings resident in Britain. If the corn-bunting has no distinctive plumage colouring by which to identify it, the cock's wheezing song, like a jingling bunch of keys, reiterated ceaselessly throughout a dusty summer's day from telegraph wire or hedge-top, often in the company of its equally ponderous mate, resembles that of no other bird, except perhaps the yellow-hammer's traditional "little-bit-of-bread-and-no-cheese." Though the corn-bunting is one of the few small birds proved to be polygamous in some

Corn-bunting, a bird with inconspicuous plumage.

49

instances—in south-west England—this is not universally, or probably even normally, the case. The cock's stuttering refrain may be heard, locally, throughout the length and breadth of the British Isles: but it is essentially a bird of the open cornlands, as it is mainly a grain- and seed-feeder and normally nests on the ground in corn or grass or brambles, though sometimes in bushes. Its haunts may be the vast open fields of southern England or the crofting strips of the Hebrides or Shetland, in which localities it is a typical bird of the townships, though absent from other islands such as Lundy or Lindisfarne. Wooded country it avoids.

Though also mainly a seed- and grain-eater, the yellow-hammer is much more a bird of

Yellow-hammer at the moment of alighting.

the hedgerow and even of woodland fringes, throughout Britain, than the corn-bunting, and nests in hedge-bottoms. The reed-bunting, on the other hand, feeds chiefly on the seeds of marsh plants and grasses, and nests on marshy ground, and is thus not generally to be found very far from water in the breeding season. In these haunts the cock may be seen clinging to a reed-stem, uttering its monotonous apology for a song over and over again, while continually spreading and closing its tail and flicking its wings restlessly. Like the yellow-hammer, the cirl-bunting is a bird of the hedgerow and hedgerow trees, nesting in these, though sometimes on the ground, and feeding on insects, grain, and berries. Its song is distinct from all other buntings' songs and includes a rattling trill which is almost identical with that of one of the summer warblers, the lesser whitethroat. It has, however, that characteristic stuttering bunting delivery and that same attitude of head thrown right back, so that the ejaculation of the simplest phrase always appears a matter of acute physical difficulty.

All these buntings are resident in Britain, but those very few snow-buntings that nest in this country are summer visitors only. Besides being the rarest of regular British breeding species, they are also much the most difficult to locate. It is possible, today, that the snow-bunting's British breeding station is restricted to one locality in the Scottish Highlands, the Cairngorm mountains; and less than half a dozen pairs may return every year, or most years, to nest under the boulders of the vast screes that spread in chaotic wastes down the steep "sidings" of those 4,000-ft. hills. In such a vast, wild, and remote country, from which for days at a time the cloud-pall never lifts, it will be appreciated that looking for a pair of nesting snow-buntings is comparable to searching for the proverbial needle in the haystack. Unless you are acquainted with a traditional nesting corrie or are so unusually fortunate as to have your attention attracted by the lark-like song of the gorgeous black-and-white cock, as he sails with raised

Cock cirl-bunting, distinguished from the hen by its prominent head streaks.

wings from one boulder to the next, your chances of ever seeing one are small. You should, however, be able to find flocks of hundreds and sometimes thousands of winter visitors and passage migrants on many stretches of sandy shore or stubble-fields on both west and east coasts, and their choral musical twittering and insect-like hissing will immediately draw your attention to their presence.

Occasional visitors to Britain include the Greenland redpoll (5 in.), which is indistinguishable in the field from the mealy red-poll; the serin (4–5 in.), a yellow-green, canary-like little finch; the northern bull-finch (6–7 in.), larger and brighter than the British bullfinch; scarlet grosbeak (6 in.) which has carmine head, breast, and rump, the female being dull-coloured with a double white wing-bar; ortolan bunting (6 in.), with greyish-green head and breast, and pinkish underparts; rustic bunting (6 in.), with rusty spotted band across silky white underparts; and the little bunting (5 in.), which resembles the female reed-bunting, and possesses characteristic copper-coloured cheeks.

Wood-lark and young at their well-concealed nest.

Industrial areas and heavily wooded country excepted, there is hardly a locality in the British Isles where the song of the sky-lark (7 in.) cannot be heard in spring and summer, from moors and even mountain pastures at an altitude of over three thousand feet down to sea-level. There will be larks singing over wasteland in English garden-cities and over the abandoned dwellings of crofters and fishermen in the remotest islands. Essentially, the sky-lark is a bird of the open spaces, whether it be Scottish moor or Sussex down, Hebridean meadow or Norfolk fresh-marsh; and nowhere can one hear such a glory of lark song as on the vast, flat saltings that stretch away to the sea's horizon in such localities as East Anglia or the Solway Firth. Because the sky-lark sings while poised between heaven and earth, and because its trilling song may be sustained, its melody unbroken, for upwards of five minutes, though commonly for two to three minutes, few other birds' songs are so widely recognized.

In most parts of Britain this recognition is correct, but in the southern half of England, especially in the south-west and in Wales, there is another lark, the wood-lark (6 in.), which also sings on the wing; though it usually does so while swinging round in wide circles, rather than while poised or mounting in tight spirals as the sky-lark. A few minutes' attention to the wood-lark's song will be sufficient to establish the identity of the singer, for while the song is sustained, like the sky-lark's, for long periods (sometimes for an hour or more at a time), it is never continuous, but is interrupted every few seconds with equally brief intervals of silence; moreover, the song-phrases are exceedingly varied, their bubbling trills recalling those of the song-thrush and especially those of the nightingale, so rich and flute-like are they, so sweet and haunting. One of the charms of the song is that it may often be heard all night, whereas the sky-lark never begins to twitter until the first paling of the dawn is faintly apparent.

Even where both larks are present in the same locality they are likely to occupy different habitats, for the wood-lark is a bird of the small field rather than the open field, and is not averse to thinly timbered country, being found in parks and felled woodlands and especially on heaths and commons. It is more of an insect and grub feeder than the sky-lark, which takes quantities of the seeds of weeds and corn. The robin may warn you that you are in wood-lark country, for the latter's call-note, *tzerwee, tzerwee, tzerwee*, is often incorporated in the robin's song. Both larks are ground nesters, the wood-lark's nest being distinguished by the inclusion of moss in its foundations of coarse grasses.

Plumage descriptions of these two larks are not very helpful, though the wood-lark is noticeably sandy-coloured with conspicuous yellow eye-stripes and a much shorter tail than the sky-lark; but there is no mistaking the only other species of lark that concerns us, the shore-lark (6–7 in.)—all the other larks on the British list being extremely rare vagrants. While the wood-lark is permanently resident in England, many of the sky-larks emigrate southward in autumn, others coming in from northern Europe to take their place during the winter. This is also true of some shore-larks, moving south from the freeze-up of their Arctic summer homes. A very few of them will winter in Britain, inhabiting the saltings, beaches, and coastal stubble-fields at a few stations between Yorkshire and Kent. So, if you wish to see these beautiful little larks, with their black and vivid mustard-yellow faces and throats and black gorgets, it will be necessary to visit one of these stations, such as Scolt Head in north Norfolk.

A wintering flock, however, may comprise no more than half a dozen individuals, and it is by no means easy to locate them as they run swiftly over the pinkish-grey mud of the saltings in search of tiny crabs and snails: for pinkish-grey is also the colour of their mantles. But their shrill tit-like chattering

White wagtail perching on a lakeside rock.

and others emigrate to southern Europe, while large numbers of immigrants or passage birds come in from Scandinavia.

Where woods or scattered trees skirt the edge of commons and moors in most parts of England, and as far north as the central Highlands, the meadow-pipit's haunts overlap those of the more stoutly built summer resident tree-pipit (6 in.). This pipit differs from the former in conducting its song-flight from and to a high perch in a tree, while the song itself is much more powerful and musical, terminating (in some localities) in a high-pitched, far-carrying *pee-pee-pee*, which forms a notable contribution to woodland song from April to July. In the autumn, when song has ended, its harsh call-note serves to distinguish it from the similarly plumaged meadow-pipit. Despite its arboreal habits, the tree-pipit nests on the ground, but builds a substantial thrush-like nest of grasses and moss in a depression.

On some stretches of rocky coast, and especially on islands, the meadow-pipit's habitat is also overlapped by that of the rock-pipit (6 in.), an exclusively coastal species, though often nesting some distance inland on the moors in island habitats. However, a pipit near rocky seashore or cliffs may usually be safely identified as a rock-pipit, except during the migratory seasons; while no other pipits are likely to be found flitting about reefs and seaweed beds, often in the spray of the breakers, in search of sandflies, sandhoppers, snails, and other small marine creatures, or nesting in cliffs or sandbanks. In appearance the rock-pipit is a bigger, darker and also greyer bird than the meadow-pipit, while its song, delivered while mounting and "parachuting," is stronger and more musical.

During the winter you may occasionally come across rock-pipits on passage along muddy estuaries and at sewage farms—which are very handy places at which to observe migrant passerines and wading birds; but you would have to be very expert indeed to distinguish these wandering rock-pipits from other migrant pipits, such as the Alpine

draws attention to them, when they make off with a dipping flight or stand, watchful, with little black "horns" erected on either side of their heads.

If voice is the surest distinction between wood-lark and sky-lark, it is virtually the only safe field characteristic of many of the pipits, those insignificant-looking, streaked and spotted lark-like birds of fields and woods, moors and seashore. The most insignificant of them, the meadow-pipit (6 in.), belies its apparent feebleness in being the most widely distributed and perhaps the most numerous of all small British birds, and must consume enormous numbers of insects. Mountain pastures to an altitude of 3,500 ft. and especially moors, where it is easily the commonest species, the remotest islands and the piece of wasteland on the outskirts of a market-town, are alike the haunts of this little bird. It continually rises from one's feet with a thin *seeping* note or mounts up a score or two feet, to parachute slowly down, with a diminishing and accelerating sequence of tinkling notes, to the vicinity of the neat little round of grasses tucked away in a tussock or in the long heather edging a moor road. In the winter, moorland-nesting pipits move down to less exposed quarters water-pipit (6 in.), which has white instead of greyish outer tail-feathers and no spots on its underparts.

Though all beautifully, and often brightly, plumaged birds, the wagtails also present considerable problems of identification in the field. All five under consideration nest in Britain, but two do so only irregularly or very locally and are more commonly seen on passage. Only one, the black-and-white pied wagtail (7 in.), with the long, ceaselessly dipping tail, will be familiar to most people as the somewhat misleadingly named water wagtail. True, it may often be seen running after insects near ponds and even tripping into the water, continually uttering its unmistakable *tzissick, tzissick,* but it is just as often to be seen on lawns and following the plough; while in the Highlands, wherever man once had a dwelling, there today you will find a pair of wagtails nesting. Even at the head of a glen, in the very heart of the mountains, you may suddenly be astonished to hear a burst of that lively warbling song, which includes many *tzissicks,* and see a wagtail sidling along the roof-ridge of the shooting-lodge. The hen-bird is no less catholic in her choice of holes in which to build her nest of grasses, moss or leaves, lined with hair or feathers; and these may be under the clod of a ploughed furrow, in stone dykes, banks, pollarded trees, sheds, or thatched roofs, and even in sea-cliffs or bombed basements in the City of London.

Though many of the pied wagtails of Britain flock together after the nesting season, establishing themselves in winter roosts, hundreds strong, in plantation and reed-beds, and even on buildings, others, including the young ones, emigrate to south-west Europe. When returning in spring they may be accompanied, especially on the west coast, by numbers of white wagtails (7 in.), on their way to their summer homes in northern Europe and Iceland, though an occasional pair will nest in Britain, sometimes interbreeding with their pied cousins. Under such conditions, and still more so in autumn, when so many of the migrants are in immature plumage, differen-

tiation between pied and white wagtails is often difficult. The sooty-mantled mature male pied wagtail is always unmistakable, and the male white wagtail, with his black cap and breast and pale grey mantle, ought to be; but it is very easy to confuse the females and young birds of the two races, though immature female white wagtails have no black on the head, as do all pied wagtails after their first autumn moult.

Similar difficulties will be experienced with the yellow (6–7 in.) and the blue-headed (6–7 in.) wagtails, but as the latter breeds in small numbers only in south-east England, you will be fairly safe in classing all yellow wagtails seen elsewhere in the breeding season as the former. This one is a summer visitor to the pastures and water-meadows of England and

Tree-pipit, which nests on the ground.

55

Wales, though scarce in Scotland, building its hair-lined nest of grasses and roots in the lush herbage. In such localities, this glowing, saffron-coloured wagtail, dancing up and down after the insects among the grazing cattle on the green fresh-marshes, cannot be mistaken for any other bird, though the hen-bird is much paler and browner; and its shrill bell-like call-note and brief warbling song are also distinctive.

The last wagtail to be considered, the grey wagtail (7 in.), is a permanent resident in Britain, though it moves southward from its summer haunts of fast-flowing streams in west and north Britain at the close of the nesting season, and you may then come across it quite often near ponds and streams in southern England. Another misleadingly named wagtail, this is the most beautiful of them all. Though its mantle is grey, all its underparts are a vivid sulphur-yellow (except that in summer the cock-bird has a little black bib), to which the eye is drawn by the constant dipping motion of its exceedingly long tail, as it trips hither and thither over the boulders in mid-stream or some near-by weed-choked spring, in pursuit of insects; or flies off with long dipping bounds, with a *zee-zee-zee* note, to its nest of moss, leaves, and roots in a crevice in an old stone bridge or in an out-

Blue tit caught in flight by the high-speed camera.

crop of rock flanking some stream or river.

Other birds which, though only rare visitors to Britain, are worthy of mention here include the dark-brown Richard's pipit (7 in.); the sandy-coloured tawny pipit (6–7 in.), which is a wagtail-like bird with long legs, and the grey-headed wagtail (6–7 in.), which resembles the blue-headed wagtail but has no eye-stripe.

TREE-CREEPER, NUTHATCH, TITS, AND GOLDCREST

With one exception all the birds considered in this section are exclusively tree-loving in their habits. They include some of the smallest birds in western Europe, the goldcrests and tits. This does not, however, prohibit them from being extensive travellers. The numbers of Continental goldcrests passing through the British Isles from and to their Scandinavian forest homes may well exceed those resident in Britain. In some autumns they swarm about the cliffs and dunes and hedgerows of the east coast; while numbers of Continental great tits and blue tits also visit the shores of Great Britain on occasions.

Yet the tiny goldcrest measures only three and a half inches from the tip of its sharp black beak to the base of its tail. Originally a bird of the pine forests, the goldcrest may now be found nesting even in gardens, still, however, suspending its exquisite hammock-nest of mosses, woven together with spiders' webs, beneath the branch of a conifer; while during the winter mixed flocks of goldcrests and tits are to be encountered swinging through the woodlands both deciduous and coniferous, in all parts of Britain, on their ceaseless hunt for spiders and insects and their larvae.

Considerable practice is needed to distinguish the goldcrest's needle-sharp, bat-like call-note from a similar one of the coal-tit's —though its equally high-pitched and persistently reiterated reeling song is unmistakable; nor, probably, will you be able to distinguish the goldcrest's greenish plumage and orange crest in the dull light of the woods. Its diminutive size, however, is sufficient identifi-

Pair of bearded tits perched on **a** *reed stem; the male has the "moustache."*

Red-backed shrikes, cock (top) and hen beside their "larder" in a hawthorn bush.

Reed-warblers; in the background is the neatly woven nest.

Goldcrests.

Spotted flycatcher.

Nuthatches.

Pair of chiffchaffs.

cation, for the only other equally diminutive bird, the firecrest (3–4 in.), is an uncommon winter visitor from western Europe to the south and south-east counties only. Moreover, as the few firecrests that do visit Great Britain tend to frequent low trees and bushes, rather than woods, the chances are that you will be able to make out the conspicuous white eye-stripe, which immediately distinguishes them from goldcrests.

There are no fewer than eight species of tit nesting in Britain, and individuals of all these except the bearded tit may be included in the mixed, insect-hunting winter flocks. The blue tit (4–5 in.) and great tit (5–6 in.) will be familiar to everyone as the most persistent visitors to bird-tables and also, very remarkably, to milk-bottles on doorsteps; and as extremely catholic nesters, building their mossy nests in holes as various as letter-boxes and hollow trees.

Not so familiar will be the coal-tit (4 in.), the second smallest British breeding bird. Its size should always distinguish it from the rather similarly plumaged great tit, while additional distinctions are a white patch on its nape and the absence of the great tit's black belly-band. The fact that all tits employ an extensive repertoire of call-notes and song-phrases makes it very difficult to set down any voice distinctions by which the various species may be reliably differentiated. Thus, though the blue tit's bell-like trilling song is quite distinct from that of any other tit, a musical ear and some experience are required to distinguish the great tit's ringing *ee-hew, ee-hew* from the similar, though actually sweeter and less metallic, *chuvee, chuvee* of the coal-tit.

The stuttering *zip-zip-zip* of a dozen long-tailed tits (5–6 in.), fluttering precariously one after another from tree to tree, is one of the most distinctive tit calls; while a tail longer than the rest of its body, and the delicate rosy tint in its otherwise rusty black-and-white plumage make this the easiest of the tits to recognize. Nor can its wonderful nest, usually placed in a bush, be mistaken for that of any other bird: for it is a large ovoid of moss

Willow-tit with grubs.

woven together with cobwebs and hair, and covered with lichens; while its lining may comprise more than two thousand feathers. Yet there is still room within the expanding walls of this curious nest for a dozen, or even a score, young ones.

All these tits are to be found in most wooded parts of Britain, except some of the more distant islands, though the long-tailed tit tends to favour copse and hedgerow rather than woods, and a characteristic haunt is a tree-lined river; while even this fragile titling may be found wandering to the last ultimate spur of pine forest nearly two thousand feet up a Highland glen.

Then there are two very similarly plumaged tits, black-capped like the great and coal-tits, which are more local in their distribution— the marsh-tit (4–5 in.) exclusively English, and the willow-tit (4–5 in.) extremely local and scattered, but extending northward into low-land Scotland. These are both stoutly built, black-and-brown tits, distinguishable only with difficulty, and often uncertainly, the marsh-tit's black cap tending to be glossy, the willow-tit's dull; while the marsh-tit has a two-noted *tzervee* call, resembling the coal-tit's, which is not included in the willow-tit's

57

Great tit leaving the nest, always built in a cavity—in trees, walls, or even pumps.

repertoire: and the latter a distinctively harsh *tchaa* note and a peculiarly rich warbling song, more suited to a canary than a tit; but here again the marsh-tit occasionally produces really musical notes. The two also differ in their nesting habits, for while both nest in holes in marsh trees, the marsh-tit rarely excavates its own holes, while the willow-tit almost invariably does; and whereas the latter merely lines its nesting hole with a thin pad of rabbit-fur and wood-fibre, the marsh-tit lays a foundation of moss with a thick pad of fur.

Finally, there is the crested tit (4–5 in.), which is found only, and extremely locally, in central Highland pine forests, where it nests in holes in rotten pine-trees. From its inseparable companion, the coal-tit, it is distinguished by its shovel-shaped, bluish-grey crest and intensely black triangular gorget, and by

parts. This bird h
meet in a broad ba

w
With the warblers
the despair, so fa
cerned, of amateur
gist alike. The Brit
than forty species,
similarly plumage
or brown birds. H
so rarely seen in
need not concern
be considered in t
either migrants or
ing in southern Eu
as the Cape. Thus
only four or five in
thousand miles to

They fall natu
inhabiting respec
rows, marsh and
group, comprising

its purring trill note, quite different from any other tit note; while its infrequently heard song is as unusual as the willow-tit's, being a sweet and brilliant little warble.

The bearded tit (6–7 in.), unlike its cousins, is exclusively an inhabitant of reed-beds and is now restricted to Norfolk and Suffolk. Even in this last stronghold it was almost exterminated by the very hard winter of 1947 and by the 1938 salt-water floods, which killed off the reeds, whose seeds provide it with its staple food in winter, though it is also an insect feeder. Like the long-tailed tit, it has an extremely long tail, and its tawny plumage immediately identifies it, while the cock-bird is further distinguished by its grey head and black moustachial stripes; nor does its "pinging" call-note resemble any of the other tits' calls. Seldom, indeed, will you see a bearded tit away from its beloved reed-beds, in which it builds its nest of dead reed-leaves low down in the bed.

With the tree-creeper (5 in.) and nuthatch (5–6 in.) we return to the woods again (and even to the bird-table), though north of the Midlands the latter is a scarce bird, whereas the tree-creeper is to be found in coniferous and deciduous woods alike from English park to remotest Highland glen. It is so well distributed that it must be quite a numerous species; but, though tree-creepers often accompany the winter flocks of tits, it is essentially solitary in habit, even roosting by itself, often in cavities in the soft bark of a wellingtonia. Its nest of moss, bark, and twigs is also inserted in crevices in bark or behind loose pieces. It must be a rare event to see more than three or four tree-creepers associating together at any season.

This solitariness, coupled with its inconspicuous habits and colouring, account for the fact that seventy years ago its song was unknown. Certainly the latter is as inconspicuous as itself, a rather louder-pitched variant of the goldcrest's, repeated at leisurely intervals, and so not attracting the ear as the goldcrest's song does by its gnat-like persistence. On the other hand, its shrill, drawn-

out *tsee-ee* is a characteristic sound of the silent pinewoods, as the little mouse-coloured bird creeps swiftly up and round the bole of a tree—its stiff tail serving the purpose of the rope round the South Sea Islander's ankles when he swarms up a coconut palm—prying its long curved bill into every crevice for insects, spiders, or woodlice. Then, with a gleam of silvery underparts, it flits down to the base of another tree and swarms up it.

In contrast to the tree-creeper, there is no mistaking the presence of the stoutly built nuthatch, with its clear thrush-like whistles and merry bubbling cries. Though it also leaps, rather than creeps, up the trunk and out along the branches, and with equal facility head-first down the trunk, its blue-grey mantle and pinkish underparts are fairly conspicuous. It might almost be described as the kingfisher of the woodlands. The nuthatch is mainly a nut eater, and particularly likes hazelnuts, wedging them in crevices and pick-axing them open with blows of its strong, sharp bill. This bill is a very handy tool, for with it the bird also plasters up its nesting hole with mud, reducing the dimensions of the entrance to a size just permitting its own entry, but keeping out larger birds, such as starlings, which might be considering ejecting the rightful occupants of the nest.

Crested tit, resident of Scottish pine forests.

59

tips to the
"waxen" t
bird is n
crossbills,
and your (
ling-like bi
top of a
strokes; a
metallic be
Of the
people kno
that nonde
coloured l
because o
branches,
which it
flights afte
hardly not
quent, soft
essentially
from all p
Scottish H

S

occasional sally out to take an insect on the wing—all the warblers being insect-feeders, though some berries are also taken. At close range in a good light, however, it is sometimes possible to compare the chiffchaff's almost black legs with the willow-warbler's pale-brown ones. This is a useful distinction when one is examining migratory warblers in coastal hedgerows, under which conditions their very different songs are infrequent and fragmentary. In their nesting woods, however, you will have to wait only a few minutes before hearing that unmistakable *chiff-chaff-chaff-chiff-chiff* . . . reiterated monotonously for several seconds at a time; or the willow-warbler's no less distinctive lisping fall of tinkling notes—the most delicately sweet and most persistently repeated of all the songs of summer. A further distinction is that whereas the chiffchaff normally places its spherical nest of moss and grass-stems a foot or two above the ground in a clump of brambles or thick undergrowth, the willow-warbler normally nests actually on the ground; while its neat domed nest is more compactly put together than the chiffchaff's, and lacks the foundation of dead leaves usually characterizing the latter's nest.

In contrast to chiffchaff and willow-warbler, the main body of wood-warblers (5 in.) do not reach Britain until late April or May; while, though widely distributed throughout wooded districts of England and Wales, especially in birch and oak woods, they become scarce in the extreme north of Scotland, wooded country being essential. The wood-warbler is easily recognized, both by plumage and by voice. The difficulty is to locate it: for though it builds a domed nest of bracken leaves and grass in a hollow on the ground, it passes the remainder of its time almost exclusively in the upper canopy of the trees, and does not sing anything like as frequently as the other two warblers. When uttered, however, its song is unmistakable, being either a stuttering ticking note which accelerates into a shivering canary-like trill or, less frequently, a swelling crescendo of a single

plaintive *tcwee* note. When seen, the bird is distinguished by its larger size and the bright colours of its yellow-green mantle, sulphur-coloured throat and breast, and pure white underparts.

The most beautiful songs of woodland warblers come, however, from blackcap (5–6 in.) and garden-warbler (5–6 in.), both of which arrive in April. Though both penetrate into Scotland and Wales, their songs are heard at their best in English copses and woodlands. In general these are by no means easy to differentiate. However, whereas a characteristic garden-warbler tends to warble on and on, in an even patter of musically perfect notes, almost without a break for upwards of five minutes, a characteristic blackcap—though also sustaining song for long periods—pours out a less even, wilder piping of wonderfully loud flute-like notes (similar in tone to the blackbird's), which terminate abruptly when the melody is at its most exuberant. In richness and vivacity the blackcap's song is unsurpassed. If a fault can be found with either song, when delivered by a good songster at the height of its song season, it is that both birds, more especially the blackcap, usually sing from dense cover, seldom perching with deliberate intent to sing. Both also nest in cover, building open nests of grass-stalks and roots, the garden-warbler's being the more strongly built of the two; but the blackcap leaves its cover much more frequently than the skulking garden-warbler and is easily distinguished, the cock having a glossy coal-black cap, which contrasts delightfully with its mate's copper-brown one. It is difficult to point to anything striking in the garden-warbler's plumage, except perhaps its notably black eye and beak and the absence of any definite yellow or green colouring.

Also nesting in thick cover, but especially in the overgrown hedgerows and rough waste-ground of fields and commons, are the two whitethroats, though the lesser whitethroat favours country including some trees for song perches. Both begin to arrive in mid-April, and from then on through the summer the

Pair of blackcaps.

Pair of whitethroats.

Sedge-warblers.

Pair of garden-warblers.

Adult mistle-thrush on a spruce branch, and (bottom) *two young birds.*

harsh "pebbly" churring of the greater white-throat (5–6 in.), from the depths of hedge or nettle-bed, and its excitable chattering warble, as it tosses itself up into the air a few feet, become a familiar feature of every dusty lane in Britain south of the Highlands. The lesser whitethroat's (5 in.) loud four- or five-note, bunting-like rattle, however, which stands out from an often inaudible warbling, is mainly a feature of the southern counties and the Midlands. Where both whitethroats are nesting in the same locality the lesser is distinguished by its blackish-grey cheeks and by the absence of the red-brown markings on the wing typical of the greater; while only the cock greater whitethroat wears a grey cap, the hen's being brown. Both nest in thick cover, a foot or two above the ground, fashioning deep cup-nests of grasses and roots: the lesser's being the smaller nest of the two.

In locating and identifying the marsh group —the sedge-, reed-, marsh-, and grasshopper-warblers—one is mainly dependent on ear, for they are all very similarly coloured, small, brown, skulking birds, seldom leaving the shelter of reed-bed or furze-clump. They advertise their presence, however, by distinctive songs and call-notes. The commonest and most widely distributed of the four is the sedge-warbler (5 in.), which disperses in May to suitable marshy places over most of Britain; thereby differing from the reed-warbler (5 in.), which is not found north of Yorkshire and Cheshire. The sedge-warbler is the less secretive of the two and, when it sidles up to the top of a reed-stem, or takes a short flight, may be distinguished by its salient yellow eye-stripe and the dark streaks on its mantle: whereas the reed-warbler is of a general reddish-brown colour, paling on the underparts to almost white at the throat. Though their songs are rather similar, being sustained for several seconds or even minutes at a burst, the reed-warbler's even and more musical warbling, while it clings to a reed-stem, lacks the extraordinary variety of harsh, musical, and mimicking notes that compose the hidden sedge-warbler's loud and forceful delivery.

The latter is liable to be provoked to song by every new intrusion on its territory, and is thus very often heard during the hours of darkness. Both nest, of course, in dense cover and usually in small colonies, the reed-warbler's deep, cylindrical cup-nest of grasses or reed-flowers being woven around any number of from two to five supporting reeds; whereas the sedge-warbler's rather bulky nest is built on a foundation of moss and dead grasses.

The third of the more or less strictly aquatic warblers, the marsh-warbler (5 in.), does not arrive in Britain until late May or June and is very local indeed, frequenting osier-beds (and sometimes uncultivated field headlands away from water) in only a few localities in the western and south-eastern counties. It so much resembles the reed-warbler that it is hardly distinguishable in the field, even by those well acquainted with it. Its full song, however, so far excels those of reed- and sedge-warblers in beauty and vivacity as to leave little doubt in one's mind on first hearing it; while, though an even greater mimic of other birds' notes than the sedge-warbler, the latter's characteristically harsh and strident notes are usually omitted. When one has been

Willow-warblers: both sexes are alike.

attracted by the song, the bird's identity can be confirmed by an examination of its nest, which is placed a foot or two above the ground. This is shallower than the reed-warbler's and is fastened to its reed or plant support by "basket-handles."

The last of the group, the grasshopper-warbler (5 in.), is less restricted to marshy habitats than the other three. In some localities in England, and more sparsely in Scotland, small colonies are to be found nesting, from late April onwards, on commons and bracken-clad sites of felled woods, hiding their nests of grasses and leaves in tussocks. This bird, too, is so skulking and secretive, and its plumage so lacking in salient markings,

that it is by its unique song that you will both locate it and identify it. Its thin high-pitched trilling reels on and on, rising and falling, as the bird turns its head from side to side, from its perch two or three feet above the ground. Sometimes it is almost inaudible, at others it carries clearly for a quarter of a mile or more. With the possible exception of the nightjar's mechanical churring it could not be mistaken for any other bird sound—though you might well suppose it to be some insect noise or even a fisherman reeling out his line.

Finally, there is the one British resident, the Dartford warbler (5 in.), which is an extremely local species, very scarce after hard winters, and an inhabitant of heaths, commons, and

Marsh-warbler at nest, always shallower than that of the reed-warbler (shown opposite).

Reed-warblers, summer residents of reed-beds in midland and southern counties.

downs in a few of the southern counties only. Building its nest of heather and grasses, with the addition of such diverse materials as thistledown, wool, moss, spiders' cocoons, and even fragments of paper, in a clump of gorse or old bushy heather, it is a secretive little bird, especially in dull weather. But on a sunny day the cock will sidle up a projecting spray of gorse from time to time, and is there easily recognized as one of the most distinctive British warblers by its slate-brown mantle and wine-coloured breast and its long fan-shaped tail, which is usually cocked up over its back. From such a perch it may utter its grating call-note or a phrase of its sweet warbling song, before diving down into cover again, to continue its search for food— spiders, insects, and caterpillars.

67

Wood-warbler near entrance to its domed nest.

European breeding birds of all these British warblers, except the Dartford, are also to be seen on passage along the coasts of Britain. In addition, there are two exclusively continental warblers, occurring at the migratory stations with some regularity, about which some notes may be helpful. The most regular is the barred warbler (6 in.), on its way south from its breeding grounds in the Baltic States to winter quarters in North-east Africa and Arabia. This is one of the easier warblers to recognize,

being a fine big bird, the size of a yellow-hammer, with distinctive tawny bars on its wings, a fawn-coloured mantle, and greyish-white underparts.

The other, also an autumn migrant to the east coast, but only in small numbers, is the tiny yellow-browed warbler (4 in.). Though hardly bigger than goldcrests, which they somewhat resemble, some individuals of this remarkable little Siberian-nesting warbler regularly get off the normal route to their winter quarters in North-east India and China. Its small size, together with its pale green mantle, whitish underparts, and pale yellow eye-stripe and double wing-bar, are sufficiently distinctive to enable the yellow-browed warbler to be identified without difficulty. Two still rarer visitors to Britain may also be mentioned. These are the aquatic warbler (5 in.), which resembles the sedge-warbler with a buff-coloured band on crown of head, and the icterine warbler (5 in.), which resembles a strongly built wood-warbler, with yellowish underparts and blue-grey legs.

THRUSHES, CHATS, ACCENTORS, WREN, AND DIPPER

All the birds in this section, except the hedge-sparrow, wren, and dipper, are thrushes and include some of the best-known and also the finest of Britain's songsters. In the early days of spring, two or three months before the warblers and nightingale return to fill the woodlands with song, mistle-thrushes, song-thrushes and blackbirds are already giving us of their superb best. The sable cock blackbird

(10 in.) with orange-coloured bill, everyone knows, though his rusty-plumaged mate is less familiar: but she, too, on alighting on garden wall or branch elevates her long tail high over her back.

The song-thrush (9 in.), with creamy breast flecked with dark-brown spots and streaks, could not be mistaken during the nesting season for any other bird except the much bigger and greyer mistle-thrush (10–11 in.), which has a characteristic swooping flight.

All three are to be found almost anywhere in Britain where cover is available in the form of trees or bushes. The mistle-thrush, however, is less widely distributed, for trees are important, both as song perches and also as nesting sites, since it usually builds its nest in a fork of a tree; where, being constructed of grasses, roots and mosses plastered together with earth, it is very difficult to see. Blackbird and song-thrush, on the other hand, usually nest in hedgerows or bushes, the former's nest being distinguished by the addition of a grass lining to the mud cup.

After the nesting season those thrushes and

Cock whinchat preparing to land

blackbirds nesting in hill country, especially in north Britain, migrate to more southerly districts, in some instances crossing the Channel. In addition, large numbers immigrate from Scandinavia, together with hordes of fieldfares and redwings. Many of these winter in Britain, while on at least two occasions a pair of redwings has been known to stay and nest in north Scotland. Ranging in flocks over fields and open woodlands, these northern thrushes pass the winter feeding on earthworms and berries. These are the staple foods of the thrush family, though mistle-thrushes and blackbirds are especially partial to fruit, while song-thrushes prefer snails, hammering their shells to pieces on favourite stones; just as the blackbird may so often be seen scratching, like a barndoor hen, among the dead leaves in a hedge bottom, for grubs and insects.

Almost as big as a mistle-thrush, the fieldfare (10 in.) wears a distinctive plumage of greyish-blue head and rump, chestnut mantle, chocolate-brown tail and streaked golden-brown breast. Moreover, its flight is direct, and there is a silvery gleam on its underparts. The redwing (8 in.) resembles a song-thrush, but as it is a confident species one can usually get close enough to it to make out its prominent creamy eye-stripe and, less certainly, the

Fieldfare perching.

russet of its flanks as bright as a beech-leaf in autumn. Neither species sings in Great Britain —though on a spring morning flocks of both, especially redwings, may be heard warbling softly in chorus with sweet linnet-like notes and liquid song-thrush trills. Both, however, have distinctive call notes, the redwing's being a woodpecker-like *pewk*, when feeding: though on migration its thin, but penetrating, "seeping" whistle is hardly to be distinguished from the still higher-pitched whistle of the song-thrush under similar conditions. The fieldfare's call is commonly a harsh chuckling *chack*: not unlike the mistle-thrush's hissing rattle; but on migration it employs an extraordinary falsetto *chisseek* call-note. But the noisiest of all the thrushes is the blackbird, especially towards roosting time on a winter's afternoon at the break of the year, when his staccato *dik-dik-dik-dik-dik-dik* rivals in persistence the pheasant's crowing from the coverts.

There is still one other true thrush to consider, the summer resident ring-ouzel (9–10 in.), which winters in southern Europe and North-west Africa, returning in March and April to hilly districts of the West Country, Wales, and especially north Britain. There it might be termed the mountain blackbird, always favouring the wildest glens and remotest ravines in the hills, indifferent as to whether there are trees or scrub in its haunts; feeding on the usual thrush diet of worms, slugs, berries and insects; and building its nest of grasses, heather and earth in a heather bank or perhaps under a juniper bush.

In less remote localities its breeding haunts may overlap those of the blackbird, and in a bad light it would be possible to confuse the two, for the white crescent-shaped gorget, which is so distinctive a feature of the cock ring-ouzel, is very dull on the hen's breast; but in either sex the rather pale greyish wings are normally very distinctive, either open or closed. Moreover, it is a bird of wild dashing flight, contrasting with the blackbird's generally weak and laboured flight. Its note is also unmistakable, being a harsh stony "chack-

Cock ring-ouzel, early spring arrival to uplands in north and west Britain.

ing." Nor is there the slightest resemblance between their songs, for the ring-ouzel is the poorest songster of the thrushes, its main song being a measured and mournful, though clear, piping *phwee-phwee-phwee*. Sometimes this is improved by the inclusion of the song-thrush's *phee-tew*, *phee-tew*, and, infrequently, by a brilliantly musical warbling phrase. The song is characteristically delivered from a boulder on the naked hillside, rather than from any prominent perch in some lone rowan tree.

Very different is the ouzel's primitive piping from the blackbird's beautiful song, than which there is no bird song more musically perfect or more mellow in tone, flute-like in quality, leisurely in delivery. However, even this superb melody may terminate in a jarring unmusical screech; while, in highland districts, where blackbirds are not very numerous, one cannot always be initially certain whether a blackbird or a mistle-thrush (10–11 in.) is

singing, so thin in tone are the blackbirds' songs. Thus, the latter assume that "remote" quality so characteristic of the mistle-thrush's sweet, clear, whistling notes flung defiantly forth from the windy top of some lofty tree. Neither song can be confused with the song-thrush's (9 in.) much varied and mimicking selection of powerful, yet crystal-clear, boy-like whistles—the song that the Englishman abroad remembers with the keenest nostalgia.

One would not on first acquaintance suspect the nightingale (6–7 in.) of belonging to the thrush family. Yet, listening to a solitary song-thrush singing from some lonely glen, you will be struck by the unexpected discovery that it is the nightingale's song more than any other of which you are reminded. But the song-thrush has no note comparable with a nightingale's magnificent crescendo-ing and ventriloquial fluting whistle, which throbs and throbs in the silent night until, if one is

71

close to the singer, one's pulsing ear-drums seem likely to burst with the vibrant waves of sound. No other bird pours forth such an unpremeditated variety of glorious notes and phrases, nor sings with such concentrated intensity, for one can shout or strike matches within arm's length of a singing nightingale without having the slightest effect on it. It must be emphasized, however, that the power, clarity, and quality of the liquid, bubbling, and superbly warbled notes vary enormously from one nightingale to another, and that a first-class performer is the exception rather than the rule; moreover, if nightingales sing for longer periods at night, they also sing very freely and more passionately by day.

Were it not for its song, the nightingale would be as inconspicuous as a garden-warbler, for in Britain it is a skulking bird, keeping mainly in the densest cover, where it spends much of its time on the ground, foraging for worms and insects; and where it also builds its bulky nest of dead leaves usually on or close to the ground. Only its croaking—so harsh and guttural a sound from so sweet a throat!—or its soft warbler-like *phuee* betray its whereabouts; and when it does take to the trees it reveals itself as a plain-plumaged brown bird with, however, an attractive coppery tail. Alas, it is mainly a

Cock wheatear with food for young.

bird of the open woodlands, copses, and hedgerows of eastern and southern England only, where it arrives in the latter half of April from its winter quarters in Africa.

In England, south of the Humber, the nightingale reaches its northerly breeding limit in Europe, but a close relative and almost as beautiful a singer, the red-spotted blue-throat (5–6 in.), replaces it in Scandinavia and Siberia, and is a regular passage migrant in small numbers along the east coast. A robin-like bird, the cock bluethroat is unmistakable with his brilliant blue, chestnut-bordered gorget; but as most British migrants are birds in immature plumage, it is not easy to distinguish them from young robins or night-ingales.

One tends to think of the robin (5–6 in.) as the most exclusively English of all birds, always at hand to snap up any worm or larvae turned up by the gardener's spade. Yet not only are there robins in almost every corner of Britain except the Shetland Isles, but, further, many of our nesting robins move south-ward in the autumn, some immature birds even crossing to Holland and France to winter. Moreover, numbers of Scandinavian robins move south in their turn to winter in Britain and as far south as North Africa. There is no need to describe the robin, except perhaps to note that the brown-spotted young robins do not acquire their russet-orange breasts until the late summer or autumn. The sweet rippling song, which is such a feature of autumn, when most other birds are songless, will also be familiar—as will the scolding "ticking" note, and perhaps that thin shrill *tsee*, which both it and the blackbird utter when suspicious but not definitely alarmed. For nesting site anything from a hole in a bank to a beam in a shed or an old kettle in a bed of nettles will suffice, though the large nest of dead leaves and moss, lined with hair, is often well hidden.

Even more closely associated with man's dwellings than the robin is a newcomer to England, the uniquely plumaged black red-start (5–6 in.), which during the past twenty-

72

Cock blackbird with hen on the nest in a *Song-thrush at the nest in a dog-rose bush; the cock is singing in the background.*

Redwing in fresh spring plumage

Pair of wheatears.

Pair of stonechats.

Pair of whinchats.

Cock redstarts with hen in tree.

five years has very gradually been extending its European breeding range to widely scattered urban and coastal areas in the southern half of England. The fact that it has become so much a feature of bombed-out areas may perhaps be due rather to its prominence in such situations than to the fact that these unprecedented conditions have attracted more settlers from the Continent. Moreover, there has always been a regular passage of European migrants through Britain, some of which have been accustomed to winter in the south-western counties. There is never any difficulty in recognizing the mature cock black redstart, whose inky black plumage is relieved only by large, though dim, white wing-patches and, when it takes flight, by the sudden revelation of that wonderful flame-coloured tail; while the greyer hen bird and young cocks lack the orange colouring on the underparts distinguishing the common redstart. Moreover, unlike the latter, the black redstart nests almost exclusively in buildings in Great Britain, feeding mainly on insects; and its brief warbling song terminates in a distinctive metallic jingling.

The common redstart (5–6 in.), though also a passage migrant, is mainly a summer resident, arriving from Africa in April and distributing itself locally over most parts of Britain except the extreme south-west and Ireland. Essentially a woodland bird, nesting in holes in trees, it is by no means conspicuous, despite its tropically bright, burnished copper plumage, being always on the move among the foliage. Indeed, it would often pass unnoticed were it not for its loud warbler-like *phuee* note, its "ticking" scold, and its sprightly and emphatic, but disjointed, warbling song, which includes fine notes of nightingale and chaffinch quality. Now and again, however, it darts out into road or glade after passing insect, affording a brief glimpse of its brilliantly contrasting colours of jet-black mask, powdered-silver forehead and French-grey mantle (all of which the hen lacks) and flame-coloured breast and tail.

The little whinchat (5 in.) is another sum-mer resident, arriving from tropical Africa late in April to take up nesting territories, locally, on commons, wasteland, hillsides and partially wooded glens in most parts of Britain. It does not necessarily demand such open country as the stonechat (5 in.), which is mainly a locally permanent, though irregular, resident in most parts of Britain from sea-shore to upland moor.

The cock stonechat, "chatting" and "wheet-ing" from the topmost spray of gorse or bramble bush, could not be confused with any other bird, with his velvety coal-black head, white lapels and wing-patch, and terra-cotta underparts; but the hen bird lacks the black-and-white effects and might be mistaken for a whinchat, if you overlook the fact that the latter has a white eye-stripe and black cheeks, and white edges to its tail, and that its underparts are always buff rather than red-dish. Their songs are also distinct, the whin-chat's being the superior, a sweet and mellow warble, including some thin notes of almost nightingale quality, sometimes reminding one of the redstart's song and at others of the wheatear's gay and volatile jingle. That of the stonechat is a simple little trilling song, recalling that of the robin or the hedge-sparrow. Both usually nest on the ground, the whinchat commonly in long grass, the stone-

Hen black redstart, an insect- and larva-eater.

73

chat at the base of a furze or bramble clump; and both are mainly insect feeders.

The last of the thrushes, the wheatear (6 in.), is also a bird of the open spaces (and a very numerous one), from grassy flats at the edge of the sea to the gravelly plateaux and boulder-strewn corries at an altitude of three thousand five hundred feet in the Scottish Highlands, being especially a bird of moors, downs, and islands. In such characteristic localities, in which it arrives from tropical Africa late in March, there is no possibility of mistaking this sandy-coloured, ground-loving bird with pale-grey mantle (brown in the hen bird) and conspicuous white rump, for any other. It is continually darting in and out of holes, or making short, low, swift flights, or bobbing restlessly about on boulders or stone dykes, incessantly flirting its black-and-white tail. It further advertises itself by its pebbly "chack-ing" note, and by its unusual habit of hover-ing a few feet above the ground with swiftly fanning wings, while uttering brief snatches of its vigorous piping, though grating, song, which includes many mimicries of other birds' songs and call-notes. In a rabbit-bury or in a chink in the dyke the restless pair will con-struct their grass nest.

Besides the nesting wheatear no fewer than nine other wheatears visit the British Isles on migration, but only one of these does so sufficiently often to warrant notice here—the Greenland wheatear (6 in.). The latter is a regular passage migrant along all the coasts and to some extent inland, on its journeys between West Africa and the Arctic islands; but a considerable acquaintance with wheat-ears is necessary before one can safely identify any large and bright-coloured wheatear as belonging to this race. Its habit of perching on buildings, haystacks and hedge-tops, while on migration, may attract one's attention initially; but this is also true of the large numbers of the common wheatear or closely allied races which pass through the British Isles to and from Scandinavian breeding grounds.

So much for the thrushes. There remain the hedge-sparrow, wren, and dipper. Though almost as common an inhabitant of gardens as the robin in most parts of the British Isles, with a distinct race in the Western Highlands and Islands, the hedge-sparrow (or dunnock) (6 in.) is often overlooked, because of its inconspicuous plumage—streaky brown, with grey head and breast—and habits, as it threads its way through the shrubbery hunting for insects, worms and seeds, or creeps about the ground beneath the bird table, rarely ven-turing to alight on the table itself. It has, however, two distinctive characteristics: the first a habit of continually shuffling its wings restlessly, and the second its loud single piping note. Its song is as inconspicuous as are its habits, being a pleasant little warbling ditty repeated several times a minute from its perch in hedgerow or bush; while its nest of twigs, mosses and grasses is built in similar situations or in a pile of brushwood or a bank.

The wren (4 in.), like the robin, needs no description, though it is more often heard than seen, having a prolonged rattling warb-ling song of astounding power and vehemence, terminating in an especially emphatic and explosive trill; besides a prolonged stuttering scold. Unlike the robin and hedge-sparrow, however, it shuns rather than seeks man's dwellings. In the remoter parts of its range, which extends to the loneliest islands of St. Kilda and Shetland (where there are distinct races), and to an altitude of two thou-sand feet in the Highland glens, it may be found nesting in cliffs and woods many miles from human settlements. In less remote regions it nests in hedges, banks, haystacks, and even sheds, the cock building an unmis-takable domed and very large nest of moss, grass, bracken or dead leaves, which the hen lines with feathers.

Though not belonging to the same family, the dipper (7 in.) is very wren-like in form, though twice as big, and equally unmis-takable. There is one other bird with a white breast, the common sandpiper, which bobs about on boulders in hill streams, but none

Cock nightingale feeding hen on nest.

St. Kilda wren, removing dropping from its bulky nest.

which also has dark brown, almost black, plumage, with a chocolate-brown head and a chestnut belly-band bordering a snowy breast; nor any other black-and-white bird with that swift, arrowy, whirring flight along the course of the stream; nor any singing bird that flies, perches, swims, and walks under water on the bed of the stream. However, the latter form of locomotion is not frequent, and the dipper's usual method of capturing small fishes and the larvae of aquatic insects is by wading in from the edge of the stream or plopping in from a boulder and submerging. The nest is also wren-like, being a large domed edifice of moss, very difficult to pick up against its mossy rock or tree-root back-ground—though the girder of an iron bridge is a favourite place—while sometimes the nest may be actually behind the curtain of a waterfall. Rarely, indeed, do you see a dipper any distance from water, always swiftly flowing rocky streams in west and north Britain; though after the young have fledged there is a general dispersal both up into the mountains and down into the lowlands. In the late autumn the birds return to take up their separate beats on their nesting streams, and one hears once again that sharp *zit-zit* of the bird on the wing or, in quieter reaches of the stream, that unexpectedly musical warbling song, from a bird bobbing on a boulder or perched on a branch just above the water.

The black-eared wheatear (6 in.), which has black wings, is an occasional visitor to Britain, as are the white-spotted bluethroat (5–6 in.), with its white gorget; and the Alpine accentor (7 in.), which is a bright chestnut colour with whitish throat spotted with black.

SWALLOWS, SWIFTS, AND NIGHTJAR

Though such familiar summer residents in Great Britain, swallows, martins, and swifts are often included together under the single title of swallow. Yet they are reasonably easy to distinguish, one from another—even in the air, where one sees them most often; for all feed exclusively on insects taken on the wing, at a considerable altitude in fair weather.

Thus, your usual view of the true swallow (7 in.) will be of a slender, dark steely-blue bird with whitish underparts and long streamers to its forked tail. You may not have time to detect that glowing chestnut-red throat and brow, as the bird dashes down to its nest in a barn, skims low over a pond, or sweeps to and fro in the upper air.

The smaller house-martin (5 in.) also has burnished blue upperparts, darker than the swallow's, and you may have difficulty in seeing its distinctive white rump when it hawks above you at some height; but its tail, though forked, lacks the swallow's streamers and its underparts are a much purer white, while its flight is noticeably slower and less erratic.

Dipper on a stone in a fast-flowing hillside stream; this is its customary habitat.

Cock nightjar yawning wide to snap up large insects, such as moths and dor-beetles.

Greater difficulty will be experienced in differentiating between the two martins, for the fawnish-brown upperparts of the smaller sand-martin (5 in.) and its only slightly forked tail are by no means easy to distinguish when the birds are hawking at any height, while its flight is very similar to the house-martin's, though more butterfly-like. However, unlike swallow and house-martin, it is not found, typically, in the vicinity of houses and likes feeding over water, especially when on migration—though this is true of the other two.

In flight the swift (6–7 in.) could only be confused with the swallow; but, except for a greyish throat, the swift is a sooty-brown bird, while those razor-edged scimitar-shaped wings, cutting black arcs across the sky at a speed of perhaps 100 m.p.h. and more, could not belong to any other bird. Nor could those noisy squealing packs of black "devil-birds," chasing at breakneck speed down the streets and in and out of the houses, or wheeling higher and higher into the summer dusk, until both they and their screaming cries are lost, be swallows.

There is, however, another swift, the Alpine (8 in.), which has wandered to Britain on a number of occasions during the summer months from its southern European home. Besides being larger than the native swift, however, it is also easily recognizable by its white undersides and pale brown upperparts.

All "swallows" found in Britain are summer residents, wintering exclusively in South Africa, with the exception of the sand-martin which winters as far north as East Africa. The latter is thus the first to return to Britain in the spring, the earliest individuals arriving before March is out, to take up colonial nesting sites in sand-pits, railway embankments, river banks and even sea cliffs, in all parts of Britain except Shetland. Soon after arriving home these little masons begin to bore the shafts of their nesting holes, clinging to the face of the gravelly bank and chipping at it with their tiny bills, eventually driving tunnels into the bank two or three feet long and an inch or two in diameter. In a chamber at the end of the shaft a rough nest of feathers and straws is made. From time to time the "builders" knock off work, to hawk around after insects or perch on a convenient telegraph wire or fence rail and twitter their small chattering, piping songs, which are hardly more complex than the harsh chirruping callnotes they utter continually on the wing.

The swallows return almost as early in the spring as the sand-martins to all cultivated parts of Britain except the extreme north; while numbers of North European breeding swallows, together with house-martins and swifts, pass up both east and west coasts. Unlike the martins the swallow is a solitary nester, constructing a saucer-shaped nest of mud and straw, open at the top, on a beam in a barn or outhouse, though sometimes in a chimney-stack. A noisy bird, it twitters continually in flight and utters piercing cries when alarmed by a cat or other intruder near its nest, which it mobs fearlessly. Its pleasant little song is warbled with great gusto both on the wing and when perched near its nest. Not unlike the sedge-warbler's song, though more musical, every phrase terminates in an emphatic whirring rattle.

The "ropes" of twittering swallows and house-martins lined up in hundreds on telegraph wires, trees, and even roofs, preparatory

Cock nightjar, his beak closed.

to setting off on their return migration to Africa, are a characteristic feature of late summer and autumn; for though the legend still lingers in rural districts, swallows do not hibernate at the bottoms of ponds during the winter, though both they and also housemartins are often to be found feeding young or roosting in reed-beds as late as October or November, while an occasional swallow may even winter in Great Britain.

It is usually well on into April before the house-martin returns and disperses to all parts of the country except the extreme north. Though today mainly an inhabitant of buildings in Britain, some colonies of housemartins are still to be found occupying those sea cliffs and inland crags which must have been their haunts before the advent of man; and, in this respect, it is interesting to find that nearly every shooting lodge in the wildest glens of the Scottish Highlands now has its small colony of martins. The house-martin is one of the master builders among British birds, its cup-shaped nest of wet mud pellets and grass stems being plastered on to the side of a wall immediately beneath the eaves, which form the roof of the nest, with a small hole at the top for entrance, the interior being lined with feathers and straw. It is also a richer and more musical, though less frequent, singer than the swallow, both on the wing and at the nest, its call-note being a peculiarly clear boyish whistle.

Last of the family to arrive and soonest to leave, it is May before the swift returns to the same districts of the British Isles as swallow and house-martin. Yet before the end of June some, perhaps non-breeding or unsuccessful breeders, are already passing south again. Being unable to perch or walk, the swift acquires its nesting materials—straws, seeds, feathers—while they are floating in the air and, carrying them to its nesting hole under the eaves or in the thatch, sticks them together with saliva to form a shallow cup. Although nesting mainly in buildings, some swifts are

Swift by its nesting-hole.

to be found in sea cliffs, and even in grouse butts on moors, while their magnificent powers of flight enable them to hawk far and wide over downs, moors and the high tops of the mountains in the vicinity of their nesting places.

The nightjar (10–11 in.) is also a local summer resident on heaths and commons, sandy links, bracken-clad hillsides, and open woodlands, in most parts of Britain except remote islands and highlands, arriving in May from its winter quarters in various parts of Africa. It is a bird you will have to seek in the dim light of dusk and dawn, for it passes the hours of daylight squatting motionless on bare ground, on which its barred and mottled grey, brown, and buff plumage renders it invisible —as it also is when incubating its two eggs in a mere scrape in the soil.

At twilight, however, the nightjar wakes up and draws attention to its whereabouts by its unique churring "song," which resembles the purring sound of a two-stroke motor-cycle, rising and falling (like running water) continuously for periods up to five minutes or more. Such is the peculiar rhythm of this churring that it is not easy to pinpoint the exact position of the bird, perched either across or along the branch of a tree; nor may the light be good enough to make out its curiously flat-shaped head and enormous hair-fringed gape, nor those striking white bars on pebble-patterned wings and tail, which distinguish cock from hen. At close range the churring is remarkably resonant, an electrical whirring, the occasional lower-pitched slurred note in no way checking the endless, even rhythm. The bird also utters extraordinary shrieks, frog-like grunts and throaty gobblings while in flight—not to mention a whipcrack of rapidly vibrating wings meeting high above its back—as it hunts its insect prey, largely moths and beetles. These noises are weird enough, at night, to account for the many legends and superstitions associated with the "goat-sucker" or "fern-owl" or "night-hawk" by country folk, as it wheels and twists and zigzags on soft-feathered

Pair of wrens and young bird (middle).

Hedge-sparrows.

Nightingales.

Pair of robins and young.

House-martins.

Adult swallow feeding young.

Dipper and young, showing their bright yellow "gapes."

pinions as noiseless as an owl, now a few feet above one's head, now sailing with incomparable grace and ease over the tree-tops, resembling in silhouette some giant swift.

BEE-EATER, HOOPOE, ROLLER, KINGFISHER, WOODPECKERS, AND CUCKOO

British birds are not remarkable for exotic plumage, but the scintillating blues and greens of the kingfisher (6–7 in.) can vie with the most brilliant colours displayed by three visitors to the British Isles—bee-eater, hoopoe, and roller.

You might see one of these three beauties once in a lifetime in Britain, but the kingfisher is always there. It is something to be thankful for, now that stuffed kingfishers in glass showcases are no longer fashionable, that this beautiful bird is well distributed and often numerous in most parts of lowland Britain where fresh water is available in the form of rivers, canals, lakes, and marsh or fen drains. Swift hill streams, however, do not know it; though, in the winter, you may often come across one in a muddy creek in an estuary or at some inland loch. But whatever the habitat, recognition is immediate and certain. When the bird is perched on a low branch over the water, the stout, plum-coloured, dagger-shaped beak, salmon red underparts, and coral-red legs and feet are easily detected. In swift whirring flight, straight as an arrow, the bird scintillates like a jewel, azure, turquoise, purple, peacock-green or the metallic green of a firefly, at the play of the light, as with piercing whistles it speeds downstream and circles back over your head.

Mainly a fish eater, the kingfisher takes up its position on an overhanging branch or on a stump at the edge of the water. When it observes a shoal of minnows or a gudgeon it plunges into the water, returning to its perch with its catch. If no suitable fishing posts are available, it will hover over an open stretch of water in a mist of fanning wings. In the bank of the stream male and female excavate a tunnel some three feet in length, which ter-

minates in a round chamber. This they line with fish-bones by way of a nest for the six or seven young kingfishers.

The bee-eater (11 in.) is really a southern European bird, but small parties of bee-eaters wander to the southern and western counties of the British Isles from time to time in the summer months. Despite their brilliant plumage—chestnut and gold on the back, bright yellow throat, greenish-blue underparts—they are more easily recognized by their long beaks and pointed swallow-like wings and tails, for their colouring tends to be conspicuous only in a good light.

The hoopoe (11 in.) is a regular-passage migrant to most coastal areas of Britain, though in very small numbers, and has occa-

Wryneck, a late March and early April arrival.

Newly hatched cuckoo, still blind, returning after evicting the first egg of its foster-parents' clutch.

Wriggling a second one on to its odd, hollow back (left) and ejecting it (right).

sionally nested in the southern counties. It builds its nest in a hole in a tree. This is one rare bird which it would be difficult to mistake, with its long curved bill, fan-shaped crest, pinkish-brown plumage, and black-and-white barred wings, and lower back. Moreover, it is equally at home in trees or on the ground.

Though the roller (12 in.) is an inhabitant of central as well as southern Europe its plumage is as exotic as the bee-eater's. At first sight you might possibly mistake it for a jay, with its blue-green plumage and chestnut back, but even in flight its brilliant turquoise wings are usually distinctive.

For so extensively wooded a country Britain is regrettably deficient in woodpeckers. However, the three species that are to be found there are handsome birds. Indeed, the green woodpecker (12–13 in.), or yaffle, is almost as beautiful a bird as the kingfisher, with its blood-red crown (black in some lights), olive mantle, and conspicuous canary-yellow rump. If these characteristics, together with its heavy bounding flight from tree to tree, are not sufficient for identification, that laughing *tew-tew-tew-tew-tewk* ringing

through the woodlands is quite unmistakable.

Parks, open woods, and the hedge and coppice country of southern England and the Midlands are typical yaffle haunts; for it is not so arboreal a bird as the spotted woodpecker and spends much of its time on the ground, stabbing its strong bill vigorously into interstices in the soil and delicately lapping up the occupants of ant-hills with its long, black, snake-like tongue. When hunting for the larvae of wood-boring insects it moves up a tree-trunk in a series of jerky hops, with stiff tail feathers pressed against the bole. At such times it will often "freeze" motionless, with head held well back from the trunk, for several minutes at a time, as if listening or perhaps watching with that peculiarly glassy eye. For nest the yaffle bores an elliptical, or almost round, entrance hole two or three inches deep in the bole of the tree, and then excavates a perpendicular shaft some twelve inches in depth, with a few wood chips at the bottom as lining.

The lesser spotted, or barred woodpecker (6 in.), has much the same regional distribution as the yaffle, though it is more local. A tiny black-and-white bird, hardly bigger

Returning for the last egg (left) *and* (right) *fledgling cuckoo being fed by meadow-pipit.*

Lesser spotted woodpecker.

varies in timbre according to the species of tree selected, and may carry any distance from fifty yards to more than a mile, in the case of the larger pied woodpecker, under such favourable conditions as a wooded hill above a lake. Though this strange "drumming" cannot be confused with any other bird sound it does resemble the natural creaking of a tree in a high wind and is extremely difficult to locate, even when the "drummer" is. near.

For nesting hole the barred woodpecker selects a decayed area in branch or bole, driving down a shaft seven or ten inches deep, with the customary wood chips for lining.

Its much larger size always distinguishes the great spotted or pied woodpecker (9 in.); moreover, its wings and back are not barred like the smaller bird's, and it has in addition a scarlet patch beneath its tail. Again, the crown is scarlet in the young birds, but the adult male displays only a large spot of this colour on its nape. Though its "drumming" sound cannot always be distinguished from the usually less powerful "drumming" of the barred woodpecker, the number of taps in each burst of "drumming" is fewer, and it continually utters a loud and distinctive *pewk*, *pewk*. Its feeding and nesting habits are more or less similar to the other's, though its nesting shaft is deeper and wider. Its distribution, however, is much more extensive, reaching as far north as the central highlands of Scotland, where it is to be found in both deciduous and coniferous woods; while from time to time small numbers of the continental race of this woodpecker visit the east coast of Britain during the winter.

During the summer the south-eastern counties in particular and a decreasing number of localities elsewhere in England are visited by another little woodpecker, the wryneck (6–7 in.). Arriving in its nesting haunts in open woodlands, orchards, wooded commons, and even hedgerows early in April from tropical Africa, the wryneck announces itself by its slow, clear thrush-like *quee-quee-quee-quee-quee*, which is more musical and prolonged and less metallic than the barred woodpecker's

than a sparrow, though stoutly built, the cock has a crimson crown. So, too, have the young woodpeckers, but not, strangely enough, the hen bird. Confining its search for wood grubs almost exclusively to the trees and often working along the underside of a bough like a nuthatch, this little woodpecker would often be overlooked in the woods did it not announce its presence by its swift and rather squeaky *pee-pee-pee-pee-pee*—which may be preceded by a querulous whinnying "screeling"—or by its "drumming."

Though the yaffle makes a loud tapping, when hammering on the bole with its bill in search of grubs, it very rarely deliberately hammers or "drums" as a means of advertisement, as both the spotted woodpeckers do throughout the spring. By hammering with extraordinary rapidity—about ten taps to every one-and-a-half-second bout of "drumming"—on a hollow part of bole or limb, which acts as a soundboard, the barred woodpecker produces a resonant booming. This

cry. Were it not for this call the bird would hardly be noticed; for though it feeds mainly on the ground, flicking up insects with its long thin tongue, it is secretive and spends most of its time in the upper canopy of trees. Its plumage, moreover, is an inconspicuous greyish-brown, mottled and streaked like a nightjar's. Though normally nesting in a hole in a tree—laying its eggs on the bare wood floor—it may also use holes in banks, walls or thatch, or even a sand-martin's burrow.

To conclude this section we have the most remarkable and most famous—or infamous— of all British birds, the cuckoo (13 in.). It is, however, as a "wandering voice" rather than as a bird that most people know him: for it is the male which *gwook-gwoo*s. Few people, except ornithologists, associate that sudden liquid bubbling cry, recalling the yaffle's pealing laughter or the curlew's skirling, with the hen cuckoo. Few probably are aware that the males also utter the most extraordinary gobblings, guffaws and cat-spitting expletives, when chasing each other or the hen cuckoo.

It is in the middle of April that the main body of cuckoos reaches Great Britain from Central and South Africa, spreading over a diversity of habitats to all parts of Britain except Shetland, and feeding on insects and their larvae, especially the hairy ones rejected by other birds. Other cuckoos pass on north to Scandinavia. Open woodlands, commons, sand-dunes, moors, and hills are alike cuckoo country, and in all places it is numerous, though especially so on moorlands, where nests most abundantly its favourite dupe, the meadow-pipit. For the cuckoo, of course, alone of British birds, does not rear her own young ones, but lays her eggs in the nests of other small birds—notably meadow-pipit, hedge-sparrow, robin, pied wagtail, and reed- and sedge-warblers. Each cuckoo lays an average of a dozen eggs in different nests of the same species of fosterer (and cuckolds the same species throughout its laying life), removing one of the fosterer's eggs in her beak and laying her own in its place. In size and colour her eggs often bear a remarkable

Great spotted woodpecker.

resemblance to those of the fosterer.

On hatching, the nestling cuckoo wriggles the fosterer's eggs or nestlings on to its hollowed back and heaves them overboard. Outside the nest the latter no longer hold any significance for their parents, whereas the vivid orange mouth of the nestling cuckoo demands food; and feed it the foster-parents do, for three weeks in the nest and subsequently after it has fledged.

That, very briefly, is the extraordinary life-history of the cuckoo. By the end of June both male and female have ceased to call and, early in July, many are already on their way back to Africa, leaving the young cuckoos to find their own way in August or September to regions of whose existence they are not even aware!

Unlike the adults, which are greyish-blue with whitish underparts barred with black, the young cuckoos are brown, with a distinctive white patch on the nape. With its pointed wings and barred plumage, the

Short-eared owl landing on nest (above), *and immature long-eared owl* (below).

cuckoo is commonly mistaken for a hawk; but its flight, though quite swift, is of a fluttering nature and lacks the characteristic beating and gliding motion of a hawk, while its excessively long graduated tail is distinctively tipped with white spots.

OWLS

Most people, ornithologists included, are much more familiar with owls as disembodied and sometimes blood-curdling nocturnal hooters than as birds; and it is by their voices that you will first discover how many different species of the five British resident owls—little, long-eared, short-eared, tawny, and barn—inhabit your district.

The best-known voice is that of the tawny owl (15 in.), often known as the brown or wood owl. This is both the most numerous and most widely distributed of all British owls, reaching the extreme north of Scotland, besides frequenting the suburbs of large towns where gardens or parks with old hollow trees are available as roosting and nesting sites. Its beautiful mellow *too-whit, too-whoo-oo-oo* hooting is heard especially on frosty moonlight nights, modulated as the bird turns its head from side to side; and it will hoot for hours outside a lamp-lit room. Coupled with its hooting is its hunting note, a staccato *kee-veck:* and very often male and female "sing" duets, the former hooting, the latter *kee-veck*ing.

The only other true hooter is the long-eared owl (13–14 in.), which, however, is much more local, with a decided preference for coniferous woods. In such localities you may hear in the early spring its soft, tremulous, yodelling *oo-oo-oo-oo-oo*. Later in the year a monotonous rusty squeaking, resembling a creaking inn sign, announces the presence of the fledged owlets. Their squeaking and their parents' answering snoring may be heard a quarter of a mile distant. The young of other kinds of owls have rather similar wheezing cries.

The real bloodcurdler, however, is the barn-owl (13–14 in.), the farmer's and marshman's owl, which utters, rather infrequently, prolonged eerie screeches. More commonly, however, it employs a snoring note and, when hunting, a sharp *tet-tet*, easily confused with a similar note of the moorhen.

The last of the common English owls, the little owl (9 in.), was introduced to Great Britain from its true home in western Europe little more than fifty years ago, and has now spread over all England and Wales up to the Border. Its mewing *wee-oo* and hunting *kee-wek* (the latter very similar to the tawny owl's call) are now familiar sounds at all hours of the day and night in agricultural country, especially in the hunting shires, and also on coastal dunes and islands.

In England the short-eared owl (15 in.) is more familiar as a winter visitor from northern Europe to coastal areas, especially marshes, sandhills and islands, than as a breeding bird; for though an occasional pair nests in East Anglia, there are no permanent colonies south of the Border counties, and the latter never contain more than a few pairs

Short-eared owl in flight.

except during seasons of vole plagues. It differs from other owls in that it is seen during the daytime and is a bird of the open country; for it searches the ground for voles and small birds during the hours of daylight, though especially at twilight; and nests in a scrape on the ground among heather or marram-grass or withered sedges. It is rather a silent owl except when its nesting haunts are invaded or when numbers are migrating together. Under the latter conditions you may have them swooping noiselessly down at your head with angry *zew-zewk*, or mobbing a kestrel perhaps with a staccato *quick-quick-quick:* while in its nesting haunts this owl circles around calling *boo-boo-boo*, intermittently dropping like a plummet while clapping its wings beneath its body. This habit of wing-clapping during the nesting season is common to most of the owls.

With its long elliptical wings and marbled pepper-and-salt plumage, and its habit of soaring and gliding, wheeling away higher and higher until lost to sight, you might well mistake the short-eared owl, initially, for a bird of prey; but it has the round face, though flat head, and the noiseless, dipping, buoyant flight of an owl. Its short ear-tufts are not a noticeable feature of its dark-brown maned head (with brilliant yellow eyes), as they are in the case of the long-eared owl. The latter, however, is so exclusively nocturnal in its habits—preying, like the short-eared, on voles and small birds—that it is rarely seen abroad in daylight. Occasionally, however, you may disturb one drawn up on its perch like a statue close against the trunk of a tree. Then it appears a greyer bird than the short-eared. It nests in squirrels' dreys or in the old nests of such large birds as magpies, crows and even herons, and sometimes on the ground at the foot of a tree.

These are also the nesting-places of the tawny owl, which, however, prefers a hole in a tree, and is to be seen rather more often by daylight. One's attention is often attracted to it by the deafening scolding of a mixed band of small birds, aided and abetted by jays, in the branches of a tree where it is roosting close up against the bole. If they chivvy it out into the open it is seen to be a dark, heavily built owl with a very large head and broad rounded wings which it flaps with slow beats. It seldom normally emerges before nightfall, however, to hunt mice and small birds; though some are unusually bold when nesting and have been known to cause serious injury to a human being with their sharp talons.

In some parts of the country barn-owls habitually hunt for voles and rats and, to a lesser extent, small birds, at all hours of the day. They fly first to one side and then to the other of drain or dyke, turning their heads from side to side, soaring up suddenly before pouncing down on a vole. In other places they are never seen abroad in the daytime. In either case the barn-owl appears at dusk as a snowy-white owl, a huge ghost-moth with round, leonine, furry head and black eye cavities; though, with the moon behind the observer, it may appear jet black. In actual fact the patterning of its mantle varies from the faintest

orange mottling to a beautiful burnished copper, shading to purplish-grey. In this respect the European dark-breasted barn-owl, which is an occasional autumn or winter visitor to the British Isles and is known locally as the blue owl, usually has buff markings on both mantle and underparts, with a good deal of grey on the former.

For roosting- and nesting-places the barn-owl favours a hole in a ruined building, church tower or dovecot and sometimes a hollow tree or even a large rabbit burrow in a cliff. It lines the hole with quantities of pellets, consisting of indigestible bones and fur which, like all owls, it casts up after a meal; for owls normally swallow their prey whole.

The little owl (9 in.) is also frequently abroad by day, hunting mainly for small mammals and insects, though in some localities small birds are preyed upon extensively. A small plump owl, the size of a mistle-thrush, with very round wings, its flight is not characteristic of its kind, being direct, speedy, and bounding. When, however, bobbing up and down on a fence or a branch of a tree, or even on the ground—on which it walks with its toes turned in like a parrot—the cream-mottled, greyish-brown little owl is unmistakable, with its very flat head and short tail, and, above all, the strikingly malevolent stare of its yellow eyes, which are framed in square white "goggles." For nest it uses a hole, whether in a tree or building or on the ground in a rabbit burrow, or under a wood stack, sometimes nesting in small colonies.

In addition to the five owls resident in Britain we must also take note of a rare visitor—the snowy owl (21–24 in.) from the Arctic. This magnificent all-white owl, nearly twice the size of the barn-owl, occurs nearly every winter in Shetland and occasionally wanders as far south as Norfolk saltings and Devon moors. A daytime owl, hunting rabbits, mice, and birds as large as partridges, it frequents open country exclusively, habitually perching on hummocks or boulders. There are several other owls, though they are less frequent visitors to Britain. These include the

Adult male bee-eater with young bird in background.

Green woodpeckers with young bird in distance; the hen is putting out her long tongue.

Great spotted woodpeckers and (top left) *a young male.*

Pair of hoopoes with their brood of young.

eagle owl (25–28 in.), which is blackish-brown, has long ear-tufts, and blazing orange eyes; Tengmalm's owl (10 in.), with an exceptionally large, round, spotted head; and the grey-brown scops-owl (7–8 in.) with ear tufts.

BIRDS OF PREY

Recognition of birds of prey presents considerable difficulties. They are usually seen in flight, often swift and at a great height, affording only a glimpse of plumage colouring, or none at all. As several species resemble each other closely, in form, plumage, and habits, it may be helpful to group them into eagles, buzzards, kite, and osprey; falcons and hawks; and harriers.

The common buzzard (20–21 in.) is often described as a small golden eagle (30–35 in.); but only if a buzzard were soaring at a very great height—and it seldom soars to the height of an eagle's station—would it be possible to overlook the magnificent breadth of an eagle's pinions, with their seven-foot span, and the long-fingered primary feathers characteristically swept up at their tips and much more splayed than those of a buzzard. Moreover, in straight flight, no buzzard ever covered so much ground so swiftly as an eagle does with a powerful flap or two. For that matter a buzzard, though continually soaring in overlapping circles, is seldom to be seen flying any distance in a direct line, but just from wood to wood or fence post to post. Further, while the eagle is an extremely silent bird, very occasionally uttering a ridiculously feeble yelp, the buzzard usually whistles a prolonged mewing *peeyowow-w-w-w* while soaring and when disturbed at the nest.

At close quarters no confusion between the two is possible, if only because of the disparity in size, the dark-brown eagle being half as big again as a buzzard, with a mighty tawny maned head and tremendously powerful hooked beak. The golden cere, or bare skin, at the base of the latter can often be seen gleaming in the sun at a great distance when the eagle is on the wing. A further distinction is that most buzzards display a greater or lesser extent of white on their underparts.

The buzzard breeds in two distinct types of habitat—sea cliffs and wooded glens or coombs; and nowhere is it more numerous than in Devon, where eight or twelve may be seen soaring at a time. It is, however, generally distributed in the western half of Britain and more widely in the Scottish Highlands. It usually builds a large nest of sticks or heather stems in a tree or on a cliff ledge, though sometimes on the ground on bushy hill slopes. A habit of constantly adding fresh greenery to its nest throughout the season draws attention to the latter. Formerly persecuted as a supposed enemy of game, the buzzard is now generally recognized as a valuable agricultural bird, preying mainly on rabbits and voles, besides, to a much lesser extent, on other small mammals and birds, snakes, amphibians, and even beetles and earthworms.

Despite its magnificent and extremely powerful proportions the eagle does not prey on large beasts and birds. Ptarmigan, those white grouse of the mountains, and Alpine hares are its ordinary prey, while in those years when hares are scarce the eaglets—commonly only one—may be fed exclusively on rabbits. Lambs of mountain sheep and deer calves are rarely killed, though occasionally one may surprise an eagle feeding on a carcass. Tolerated in deer forests, though not on grouse moors, the eagle is holding its own in the more mountainous glens of the Highlands and may be repopulating south-west Scotland. Gaelic place-names show that some traditional eyries have been occupied for centuries, though the eagle wisely varies its nesting place from year to year, using two or three alternative eyries—on craggy ledges or in pine trees—several miles apart. The actual nest is an enormous platform of branches or heather stems or bracken, which will support a man's weight, for the eyries are often easy to reach.

In the unlikely event of your seeing a white-tailed eagle (27–36 in.) or sea-eagle, its short white wedge-shaped tail may be prominent; but one must bear in mind that not only has

Sparrow-hawk, watching over her young at the nest.

90

the immature golden eagle a white bar across its tail, but also that the immature sea-eagle's tail is dark brown. An eagle seen on the east or south coasts of Great Britain, however, is almost certain to be a sea-eagle which, in addition to mammals and birds, also preys on fish. Until the nineteenth century this eagle had eyries in many parts of the British Isles, the last pair nesting in Shetland in 1908.

You are not very likely to see rough-legged buzzards (20–24 in.) or honey-buzzards (20–23 in.) either, though most winters one or two of the former find their way to Britain from northern Europe. Most rough-legged buzzards are whiter than common buzzards, often so snowy white as to be visible as a white dot on the hillside a mile distant; moreover, their tails are white and their legs are clothed with white feathers down to the base of the toes. More terrestrial than the common buzzard, they may be watched running quite fast over the ground.

The honey-buzzard, which was formerly a rather rare resident in England, especially in the New Forest, but now nests only irregularly, is as variably plumaged as the other buzzards; but, both in flight and when perched, it appears longer and slimmer, with a number of broad dark bars on the underside of its tail.

To see the kite (20–25 in.) in Britain you would have to make a special journey to a solitary haunt in the hills of mid-Wales, where a very few pairs continue to breed year after year under the strictest protection, building their nests in tall oak trees. These are the last survivors of the thousands that scavenged the streets of towns and villages throughout Britain five hundred years ago. Though somewhat buzzard-like in appearance, in voice, and in its habit of soaring for hours together, the kite is immediately distinguished by its long deeply forked tail and long, narrow, angled wings, while its dark reddish-brown plumage, with black primary feathers, lacks the whitish mottling and streaking of buzzards.

Though the osprey (20–23 in.) nested on Scottish lochs until the early years of this cen-

tury, it too has suffered the fate of so many of the finest birds of prey, and today is no more than a rather rare bird of passage, although a pair has recently nested again in Scotland. Though about the same size as a buzzard, it cannot be mistaken for any other bird of prey, because of its contrasting plumage of dark-brown mantle and pure white underparts; moreover, its head is whitish with a dark band at the side. Having the distinction of being almost exclusively a fish eater, plunging into the water from a height after its prey, it is usually seen near lake, fen or estuary, even when on migration.

The various species of falcons and hawks are more difficult to differentiate and, to complicate matters, male differs from female in every instance. It is all very well to state, for example, that a peregrine (15–19 in.) may be half as big again as a merlin (10–13 in.), with the hobby (12–14 in.) intermediate between the two; but in actual fact a large hen merlin is not very much smaller than a small peregrine tiercel, as the male is called; while, in flight, size is no criterion at a distance, and all three have that same "winnowing" action of rapid wing-beats varied by long glides. Moreover, their high-pitched, "whickering," screaming cries sound very similar to anyone not well acquainted with falcons. For the novice the safest distinctions are to be found in each species' distinctive habitat and method of taking its prey.

Mention must also be made of a large peregrine from the Arctic, the Greenland (21–24 in.). This is a magnificent white falcon with black mottlings and streakings, which is fairly common in Scotland and Ireland.

The peregrine is an inhabitant mainly of sea cliffs in south and west England, with the addition of inland crags in hilly country over the rest of Britain. It nests on bare ledges or in holes in cliffs, sometimes taking possession of the old nests of such neighbours as ravens and crows. It preys far and wide on numerous species of bird—the favourite, however, being pigeons—which it kills either by striking in a power-dive, with wings folded to sides, at a

Hobby and young at nest, always one vacated by other birds.

speed and momentum which must be seen to be believed; or by striking or "binding" to its victim in straight flight.

The merlin usually flies its victim down, following its every twist and turn and mounting a few feet above it before striking; for its prey is mainly small birds, especially the meadow-pipit, which is the most numerous inhabitant of the moors, bogs, and coastal dunes that are the merlin's haunts in Wales, north England and Scotland, though a few pairs breed on Exmoor and Dartmoor. Unlike the peregrine, the merlin usually nests on the ground, either in a bare scrape or in a rudimentary nest of heather stalks or bents. When nesting in cliffs or trees, however, the former nest of a crow is utilized.

The hobby is the falcon of open woodlands predominantly in the south of England, old nests of squirrels and crows, magpies, jays, sparrow-hawks and other birds being annexed. In the south it usually nests in pine trees, but in deciduous trees in the Midlands. In pursuit of its prey the hobby adopts the methods of the peregrine, displaying marvellous agility and speed in capturing such masters of flight as dragon-flies, swifts, and swallows.

It will be clear, then, that peregrine and hobby occupy different regions and habitats, and that you are unlikely ever to see the two together; whereas peregrine and merlin often overlap, both in their breeding haunts and also in their winter quarters on coastal saltings and fresh marshes. In the latter haunts their numbers are augmented by others, almost exclusively brown, immature birds, from northern Europe. In all cases it is worth bearing in mind that the merlin lacks that dark moustachial streak, characteristic of peregrine and hobby at all ages.

At close quarters the peregrine's size is sufficient guide to its identity. It is a blue hawk: the falcon being darker and browner with heavier black bars on her pale underparts. The hobby resembles a small slim peregrine with, however, rusty-red thighs and undercoverts. The male, or jack, merlin is a little slate-blue hawk with reddish-brown coloured underparts: the hen merlin is dark brown.

At rest the hen kestrel (13–14 in.) might be confused with the hen merlin, though the former is a ruddier brown; but the cock kestrel has a distinctive bluish-grey head, rump, and tail. Much of a kestrel's life, however, is passed in conspicuous hovering flight on swiftly fanning wings, while it searches the ground below for vole or grasshopper.

In contrast to the kestrel and other falcons, whose wings are pointed and scythe-shaped, the sparrow-hawk (11–15 in.) is a round-winged bird with a long tail; while its method of hunting is to dash low through the woods and skim the hedge-tops in pursuit of its small bird prey. The cock is a slate-grey bird with reddish-brown barred underparts; the hen is much bigger, browner on the mantle, and whiter beneath.

The kestrel is the most numerous and most widely distributed of all British hawks, occurring in every type of habitat except industrial and heavily built-up areas throughout Britain, from coastal marsh, through woodlands and moors to an altitude of three

Rough-legged buzzard, passage migrant and winter visitor to Britain.

thousand feet in mountainous districts. Like other falcons it nests in scrapes on cliff ledges, other birds' old nests in trees, or hollows in trees and buildings. In autumn and winter immigrant kestrels from northern Europe swell the numbers of residents, especially on fresh marshes, where their squealing *kee-lee-lee* is to be heard the day long.

The sparrow-hawk is essentially the hawk of woodlands and agricultural country in most parts of Britain, usually building its own rather large nest of twigs close up against the trunk of a tree, though sometimes using old nests of other birds as a foundation platform. Its presence in its nesting haunts would probably pass unnoticed were it not for its habit of soaring high over the wood with a loud *squee-oo* cry.

Finally there are the harriers, which are large kestrel-like birds with very long wings and tails, and a habit of quartering low over the ground with a flapping flight as buoyant and leisured as an owl's, pouncing down on their prey from time to time with agile banks and turns. Their rounded heads are also rather owl-like. Only the expert, under favourable conditions, can distinguish between the females of Montagu's harrier and the hen-harrier; but as the former is a scarce summer resident in southern England, and the latter an equally scarce resident in north and west Scotland and a winter visitor to other parts of Britain, the possibility of confusion seldom arises. There is a remarkable contrast in the male and female plumage of these two harriers. The cocks are beautiful pearl-grey birds with black-tipped wings, Montagu's being distinguished by a dark bar across the wing; while the hens and immature birds are brown with a distinctive white patch on the rump and prominent dark bars on the tail; the immature Montagu can be distinguished by its reddish-brown underparts. It is these immature "ring-tails," as they are known, that are most commonly seen during the time

Hen-harrier and young at nest. Always constructed on the ground.

they are on autumn passage in Britain.

Montagu's harriers (15–18 in.) tend to breed in scattered colonies in such diverse haunts as reedy marshes, heaths or moors, where they nest on the ground in thick vegetation, building a nest of rushes or coarse grasses, and preying on frogs and toads, snakes, voles, small birds, and their eggs. Being rather silent and secretive birds (as is also the hen-harrier), a small colony of Montagu's may exist for some years before being discovered.

The few pairs of hen-harriers still breeding in Britain do so on remote moors, preying more commonly on small birds, rabbits, and voles than the Montagu's. Their nests consist of a thick lining of rushes or grasses in hollows in the ground.

The marsh-harrier (19–22 in.), which is an extremely scarce, though increasing summer resident in East Anglia and one or two other districts of England and Wales, is larger than the other two, with more rounded wings. Moreover, both cock and hen are dark-brown with pale yellowish heads and shoulders; the cock being distinguished by grey bands on wings and tail. Its haunts are the dense reed beds characteristic of the Norfolk Broads. In these it builds a large nest—much larger than those of the other harriers—of dead reed stems and various other water plants; and, when seen, it is usually quartering just above the tops of the reeds, hunting for frogs, toads, or snakes, or small birds, or mammals. If you are lucky, however, you may witness the aerial display of the cock harrier, in which it soars and dives and rolls, even looping the loop, to the accompaniment of a high-pitched *weeoo* cry.

STORKS, SPOONBILL, IBIS, HERONS, BITTERNS, AND FLAMINGO

These are all long-legged and long-necked birds found mainly near water, and introduce us to the birds of the marshes and coast. Only two of those mentioned in this section, the common heron and the bittern, breed in the British Isles, and only the former is generally

Hen-harrier in flight.

distributed throughout the whole country.

On an average some four thousand pairs of herons nest every year in England and Wales, and considerably fewer in Scotland. Their numbers are much reduced in very hard winters, but are quickly brought up to strength again, possibly with the addition of some of those immigrant north European herons which winter in Great Britain.

The characteristic view of a heron (36 in.) is of a tall, gaunt, grey bird, with a long, thin, yellowish neck, black-plumed head and long, yellow-brown, dagger-shaped beak, peering over the top of reed bed, river bank, marsh dyke or mudflat creek; or poised, motionless, with an S-shaped kink in his neck, waiting to make a lightning strike at passing fish, which he does with a sudden uncoiling of that sinu-

95

ous neck and an excited lifting of great wings. Tilting back his snaky head, he swallows the fish with a gulp, or, if it be a large one, stalks thoughtfully from the water and beats it two or three times on the bank before swallowing. Often, however, he stalks through the shallows, stirring up eels from the muddy bottom; while frogs, water voles and field mice are also speared.

The queer thing is that the heron and many other long-legged wading birds nest in colonies in the treetops; so that in the breeding season, during the six months from February to July, you will also find herons as much as five miles from the nearest marsh or river. In wilder country they sometimes nest on cliff ledges above sea lochs and even on the ground on islands. The colonies may be of any size up to a maximum of a hundred pairs or so, and several nests may be built in one tree. The nests are built of branches and twigs; and, if not destroyed by winter gales, may in the course of time become of massive proportions.

Standing beneath a heronry one hears the most extraordinary croaking, screaming,

Purple heron, an uncommon visitor to Britain.

chittering, rasping cries, and especially a resonant booming *hoop* from the nesting birds, which are continually arriving and departing. Away from the heronry, however, and during the autumn and winter, the characteristic note of a heron, especially at night, is a harsh rasping *waatch* or *krank*, as the alarmed bird stretches upward into flight, with long shanks hanging; or as it passes across country at a considerable height to its fishing grounds, with a slow, even, heavy flapping of its enormous arc of wings, head hunched into shoulders, long legs stretched out behind short square tail.

The purple heron (31 in.), a somewhat smaller and even thinner heron, is a rare summer wanderer from western Europe to the east coast of Britain. Even at a distance its plumage may show up noticeably darker than the common heron's, and it may also be possible to distinguish its very long toes. At close quarters its mantle and wings are a dark slaty-grey, contrasting with the heron's French-grey plumage, and its bronzed neck has bold black stripes in place of long black-and-white plumes.

Equally rare visitors, mainly in the summer months, from southern and western Europe, are two small herons little more than half the size of the British ones—the squacco (18 in.) and night herons (24 in.). The former is a very pale brown bird at rest, and may appear white in flight, as its wings and tail are of this colour. The latter is a stocky, bull-necked heron with black crown and blue-black mantle, grey, rounded wings and tail, and greyish-white underparts. In form it resembles a bittern rather than a heron, though bitterns are brown birds with black streaking and mottling.

Unless you happened to come across an immigrant, the haunts in which you are most likely to find the bittern are the East Anglian broads and Cambridgeshire fens; for during the past thirty years bitterns have been nesting in increasing numbers in the dense reed beds of these localities. During the early spring and summer your first indication that there are

Pair of kingfishers perched on a stem of sedge.

Male cuckoo and, in the background, young bird being fed by a pied wagtail.

bitterns about is likely to be their booming, especially in the twilight of dusk and dawn. This extraordinary resonant booming of the cock bittern, which is usually repeated three or four times, may be heard more than a mile distant. This may well be your closest acquaintance with the bird, for it spends most of its time in the reed jungle, and fishes mainly at night in the shallow water among the reeds. Occasionally, however, one may be seen flying a short distance just above the reeds, when, with its slow-beating, curved and tapering wings and pale underparts, it somewhat resembles a large, heavily built owl—though its legs stretch out behind its short tail. Should you come suddenly upon one near its nest in a reed bed, it will "freeze," extending its long pointed beak and thick neck upwards, until the latter appears almost as thin as the reeds, which its striped underparts much resemble. Its loosely constructed nest of reeds and other water plants is built on a foundation of roots just above the level of the water.

Another bittern, the little (14 in.), is only a rare visitor from western Europe, though it has probably nested occasionally in East Anglian reed beds. It is only half the size of the native bird, and is a much paler brown, the male having a black back and black and white wings.

Though also very rare, the American bittern (26 in.) has been recorded on a surprising number of occasions during autumn and winter, at which seasons it migrates southwards to central America. It much resembles the British bittern, but is slightly smaller and is freckled instead of boldly mottled and streaked.

The glossy ibis (22 in.) is much more like a black round-winged curlew than a heron. It is a central and south European bird. Small parties of ibis visit the south and east coast mudflats of Britain in most years, especially in the autumn.

It is curious that the white stork (40 in.), so famous in Holland and Germany, should be such a rare wanderer to Great Britain in

spring and still more infrequent in autumn. A long-necked white bird, rather larger than a heron, with mainly black wings and red legs and beak, it is easy to recognize; and, unlike the heron, it flies with neck stretched out.

The spoonbill (34 in.), on the other hand, is a regular spring and autumn visitor to the eastern and western counties, sometimes wintering in south-western estuaries. Holland is today its nearest breeding ground. About the size of a heron, the spoonbill is an all-white bird, greyish-white on a dull day; and even when flying at a considerable height, with long neck and legs stretched out, the remarkable flat disk-shaped tip to its long spoon-shaped bill can usually be distinguished. Its broad "hollowed-out" wings beat rather more rapidly than a heron's, with occasional brief closures.

Occasionally seen in Britain are the black stork (38 in.), which is black with white under-

Night-heron, a visitor from Europe.

Spoonbills, which until the seventeenth century nested in Britain; they are now only migratory visitors.

parts; and the flamingo (50 in.), which has an extremely long neck and legs, a white body, and black-and-scarlet wings.

SWANS, GEESE, AND SHELD-DUCK

Perhaps it is the beauty and wildness of their haunts that make swans, geese, and ducks the favourite study of many naturalists; or is it their extraordinarily interesting habits or their beautiful plumage? Swans and geese in particular have a grandeur absent in all other birds except the larger birds of prey. Grandest of them all, so far as size is concerned, is the mute swan (60 in.), the characteristic semi-tame swan of every English lake and ornamental pond, but also a genuinely wild bird in many parts of the country. The mute is always in Britain, but during the winter two other north European swans are to be found there.

Of these the whooper (60 in.) is especially common on lochs, bogs, and mudflats in Scotland and north England, sometimes in herds of hundreds, but more commonly in family groups of thirty or forty. A few pairs, indeed, nest regularly in the Highlands. About the same size as the mute swan, though more squat and heavily built, the whooper may be recognized by its goose-shaped head and commonly straight neck, which never assumes such graceful curves as the mute's, and by its straight bright yellow beak, which is so unlike the mute's orange beak with prominent black basal knob. Moreover, the whooper is a talkative bird and its musical medley of trumpeting notes (not at all unlike those of the cuckoo) draw attention to it at a distance, whether when feeding or when on the wing, whereas the mute swan usually only snorts and hisses. On the other hand, whereas the latter's great wings produce a rhythmic musical clangour in flight, the whooper's only swish. The latter, incidentally, never "busks" its wings as the mute constantly does at breeding-time.

Except in Ireland, where herds of several hundred occur, Bewick's swan (48 in.) is normally an uncommon winter visitor from the frozen Zuider Zee, appearing most frequently in hard winters in similar habitats to the whooper. Though actually much smaller than the latter, this disparity is not always apparent; while its loud trumpeting *phow-o* might also be confused with the whooper's softer *gwuck-gwoog* by the novice. Size apart, the safest distinction at a reasonable distance lies in the Bewick's beak, which is mainly black, whereas the whooper's is mainly coloured yellow.

All swans feed mainly on water weeds, which they dredge up from the bottom with their long necks. In this way, too, the mute swan acquires the material for its enormous nest, which may be heaped up in the shallows, on an islet, or on some place near water. Like

Mute swan and cygnets on the Thames, near Maidenhead.

White-fronted goose, a winter visitor.

the whooper it is normally a solitary nester, but in the vast swannery at Abbotsbury in Dorset there are several hundred pairs.

You should not experience great difficulty in distinguishing the three British swans, but the five species of grey geese wintering in Britain can be confused by the most expert wildfowlers and naturalists, despite the fact that they are noisy birds. In the summer, from about late May to early September, the odds are that any grey goose is likely to be

Barnacle-goose, which nests in the Arctic.

the grey lag-goose (30–35 in.), for it is the only British resident, a decreasing number of pairs breeding in north and west Scotland. They nest on moors or on islands, constructing nests of long heather stems, bents, and mosses, together with down and feathers. Both in appearance and voice the grey lag resembles the old English farmyard goose, of which it is the ancestor; that is to say, it is a heavily built, greyish-brown goose with (like all grey geese) much white on the tail, above and below, a stout orange-yellow beak and long flat head, and pink legs. Its feeding habits are also those of the domestic goose, for it is mainly a grazer of short grass.

In the autumn a few thousand additional grey lags from Iceland and Scandinavia come down to winter on fresh marshes and saltings in small flocks of a score or hundred or two, mainly in north-west England and the Solway Firth. But other grey geese also come down from the high north to winter in similar habitats and localities. By far the most numerous and also the most widely distributed of these is the pink-footed goose (24–30 in.), which nests in Greenland, Iceland, and Spitsbergen. In the west of Britain its haunts are those of the grey lag; but large numbers also winter on estuaries up and down the east coast, flighting inland to their feeding grounds on stubbles and potato fields; for they are grain and root feeders rather than grazers like the grey lag, and guzzle at the roots rather than snipping off the shoots. A salt marsh that has been worked for plantains by a flock of several thousand pink-feet is pitted with holes, as if a herd of small pigs had been snouting around. They are a gregarious species and like to feed and roost (on some sandbank well out in the estuary) in large numbers. Any flocks of grey geese more than five hundred strong in these districts are, therefore, almost certain to be pink-feet.

Moreover, while the grey lag is a noisy goose on migration when, like all geese, it flies in shifting V-shaped skeins, it tends to be rather silent at its feeding grounds; whereas small or large gaggles of pink-feet are continually getting up to fly round with a babel of yelping metallic cries, which might be rendered *gug-gug*, *queek*, *queek-queek*, *quick-quick-quick*, *quank-quank*. These are higher pitched than the grey lag's honking and deep clanging *owch-owch*. So far as appearances go distinction between the two is comparatively easy on the ground, for the pink-foot is a smaller goose than the grey lag and is browner, especially on head and neck, with a conical head and a stubby bill, which is black with a pink band. On the wing and on migration, when flocks of pink-feet rarely include more than a couple of hundred individuals, recognition is uncertain to all except those with a good memory for voice distinctions, though the grey lag's wings do appear much broader and their bluish-grey colour is often apparent.

The bean-goose (28–35 in.), the brownest of the grey geese, might be described as a large pink-foot, though its legs are orange, whereas those of the pink-foot are puce-coloured, and its long beak is black and orange-yellow. The amount of black on the beak varies, and the majority of bean-geese visiting Britain from northern Europe are of the yellow-tipped type. But they occur in small and scattered flocks only, mainly in the eastern counties and south-west Scotland, frequenting pastures and marshes, rather than stubbles. They are the least vocal of all geese, seldom uttering more than a low bleating honk; and their silent habits are a clue to their identity when on migration.

Last of the grey geese wintering regularly in Britain is the white-fronted goose (26–30 in.) from Arctic Europe and Greenland. Both in voice and appearance it is the easiest to recognize, for the adults display white patches on their brown foreheads and are heavily barred with dark-brown on their dark-grey bellies, their beaks and legs being orange. In this respect, however, it must be noted that some grey lags also display this dark barring on the underparts, and others a certain amount of white on their foreheads. On the wing the white-front is further distinguished by its unique call, a husky quavering, almost

Grey lag-goose, a British breeder.

laughing *corr-rr-lew*. Its winter haunts are also rather different from those of the other geese, for it is more partial to water meadows and bogs than to fields and stubbles, and it is essentially a west coast bird from the Severn to the Hebrides, flocking together in thousands to the great Irish slobs and to the New Grounds on the Severn, though small flocks occur in many parts of Britain, often well inland.

Another white-fronted goose, the lesser

Whooper swan, which nests in the Highlands.

Bean-goose, which breeds in the Arctic Circle.

the extremely high pitch of its call-note.

Then there are three species of black geese. Only one of these, the resident Canada (36–40 in.), occurs inland. Originally introduced, the Canada goose now leads a wild life in many parts of England, Wales, and south Scotland, frequenting marshes and pastures in the vicinity of lakes and meres, and nesting in small colonies on islets or marshy land. Largest of the British geese, it is brownish with a black head and neck and extensive white cheeks. It is further distinguished by its loud trumpeting honk.

The only goose with which it could be confused is the barnacle (23–27 in.), whose breeding grounds are located in Greenland, Spitsbergen, and Novaya Zemlya; but the barnacle is only half the size of the Canada, with a grey mantle and velvet-black neck and breast contrasting with snowy white face and belly; while the chorus of a flock of barnacles sounds like the yelping of a pack of beagles. Moreover, it is exclusively a coastal goose, frequenting salt marshes, links, and grassy islands mainly in the Hebrides, Solway Firth, and Ireland; and grazes predominantly on grassy swards and such favourite marsh plants as the glasswort.

The third and smallest of the black geese, actually no larger than a sheld-duck, though with an enormous breadth of wing, is the brent goose (22–24 in.), of which there are two races, breeding in various localities of

(21–26 in.), has until recently been regarded as an extremely rare vagrant to Great Britain from northern Europe and Siberia. Closer study of the large flocks of white-fronted geese now suggests, however, that it may visit Britain more frequently than previously supposed. Apart from its small size, which, however, is not a safe criterion in the field, it is also distinguished by the greater extent of the white marking on its head and also by

Canada geese, a species introduced to Britain from North America two centuries ago.

Arctic Europe and Asia. Both winter on all coasts of Britain where there are tidal mud-flats, feeding on the long zostera weed, which grows in luxuriant beds on the mudbanks. Sometimes you can watch them feeding close up against the sea-wall; but unless you go after them in a punt, your usual view is a distant one, when they appear to be black geese with white tails and underparts, though one race is much darker on the belly. You may hear their guttural croaking chorus when their long black columns stream in from sea to the mudflats, for they are the noisiest of all geese. At close quarters they are distinguished from barnacles by their sooty-black heads and necks, relieved only by a small white nick at the side of the neck.

Before going on to deal with the large number of British ducks we have to consider the sheld-duck (24 in.), which displays characteristics of both ducks and geese. It is resident in most parts of Britain where there are estuaries or sand-dunes, while during the breeding season it may also be found some miles inland on dunes and commons, where it nests in rabbit burrows and sometimes in stone dykes or under bushes. A large pied, though predominantly white, duck with a velvet-black head, dark chestnut shoulders and belly-band, and black-tipped wings and tail, it is easily recognized at any distance; while at close range—and it is not so shy as most duck—it is further distinguished by magenta-coloured beak and legs, the former prominently knobbed in the larger drake during the breeding season. Its voice is also characteristic, with whistling *tsew* and raucous *argg-argg-arrg*, and it has a distinctive method of feeding, in which it sweeps its beak to and fro or dredges it through the mud, sifting the ooze for small mollusca, crustacea, fish, and lugworms.

Two rare visitors to Britain are the snow-goose (25–28 in.), which is pure white, whereas albinos of other species of geese tend to be cream-coloured; and the orange-brown ruddy sheld-duck (25 in.), which shows white on wings in flight. It is not to be confused

Sheld-duck beside a salt-stream.

with the ornamental Egyptian goose occurring in a semi-wild state in East Anglia.

DUCKS

Ducks can be grouped broadly in three classes—those, such as shoveler, gadwall, pochard, and tufted duck, which are almost exclusively freshwater duck; those, such as mallard, teal, pintail, wigeon, goldeneye, goosander, and smew, which are to be found on both fresh and salt water; and finally the out-and-out sea-duck, the merganser, scaup, eider, common and velvet scoter, and long-tailed duck. The reservation must be made, however, that while none of the sea-duck will normally be found inland except during the nesting season, all the "freshwater" duck may be seen from time to time on mudflats and estuaries.

Most numerous and widely distributed, from town ponds to the remotest corners of the British Isles, is the mallard (23 in.) or wild duck. Though nesting mallards are resident their numbers are augmented in winter by enormous flocks of immigrants from Europe. As the familiar ancestors of farmyard ducks,

103

the handsome green-headed drake and brown duck need no description, except perhaps to note that the hoarse quacker is the duck, the drake's call-notes being a low murmuring or thin whistling. Feeding mainly by night, on that variety of vegetable and animal matter common to all freshwater ducks, the mallard, like the teal and the wigeon, is one of the flighting duck, proceeding at dusk from its resting place on lake or woodland pond to its feeding grounds in ditches, marshes, and estuaries. The duck normally builds her nest of down and dead leaves on the ground in thick cover, though sometimes in trees.

Though the mallard drake is unmistakable, his duck could be confused with those of the gadwall, shoveler, or pintail. Drake and duck gadwall (20 in.) are rather alike, the former being greyish and the latter brown, both having whitish underparts. In flight the black-and-white patch, known as the speculum, on their wings is a means of identification, for the mallard's is purple-blue and white, while when at rest the drake gadwall (though not the duck) shows black above and below its tail. Voice distinctions are not very helpful, as the gadwall duck's quack resembles the mallard's, though it is less raucous, while the drake's croak is seldom heard. However, though a resident, winter visitor and passage migrant,

Pintail (drake).

the gadwall is a distinctly local and uncommon duck, breeding regularly at only one reservoir in East Anglia and in some Scottish localities, where it makes the usual nest of down and vegetable matter in thick cover close to water.

The pintail duck (26 in.), another silent one, is most easily distinguished by its upright carriage and slim form when swimming, and by its long, slender neck and pointed tail and wings in flight. The grey drake is unmistakable, for besides being the "greyhound" of the ducks from long neck to "pintail," and perhaps the swiftest flyer of them all, a distinctive white stripe runs down its dark-brown head and neck to join the white breast. Very few pintails breed outside Scotland, where they nest on the ground in small colonies on shores and islets of lochs. As winter visitors and passage migrants, they, like the gadwall, occur commonly in single pairs or small flocks only; though flocks of several hundred are sometimes encountered on the coast and in estuaries, where they are more often seen than inland. Their feeding places are on fresh marshes inland and on saltings and mudflats on the coast, and their food, which they obtain mainly at night, comprises grasses and plants of various kinds (including the marine zostera), which they obtain by "up-ending" and reaching down with their long necks.

The shoveler duck (20 in.) is more easily distinguished by her huge spatulate bill, heavy build and pale-blue forewing; while the drake is a striking bird with a gleaming dark-green head, white breast and chestnut belly. Though breeding shoveler may be summer residents only, their kind are to be seen throughout the year, as continental birds visit Britain on passage and to winter. Since it feeds by dabbling that huge beak in water and ooze, sieving out small animals and water plants, the shoveler requires shallow waters in which to feed, and is therefore commonly to be found in the vicinity of reedy marshes, water meadows, or bogs. In these it also nests in open situations, lining a hollow on dry ground with grass and down; and may be

104

Little owl clutching a short-tailed field-vole; behind are the nearly fledged young.

Tawny owl, also known as the brown owl, with young.

Barn-owl and young at the nest in a dead tree.

Long-eared owl and young of about a fortnight old.

found breeding locally in most parts of the British Isles, though usually solitary or at most a few pairs together.

The wigeon duck (18 in.) is another brownish, sober-plumaged bird, rather smaller than any mentioned thus far, and with a slightly conical dark-crowned head and stubby bill, white underparts and short pointed tail. Once again, the drake is most strikingly plumaged, whether in flight or on the water. A pale-grey duck with yellow-crowned chestnut head and lavender-coloured breast, its white underparts and wing-patches are very prominent in flight. It is one of the easiest to recognize at a distance, because it continually whistles a loud musical *wrr-ee-oo*, while the duck purrs and *chockaw-rrs* in reply. Though probably not as numerous as mallard, wigeon commonly associate in flocks of hundreds or thousands during the winter, when vast numbers immigrate from the Continent, and their evening flight from sea or estuary waters to their feeding places on grassy saltings or mudflat zostera beds is a feature of winter on the coast; but large numbers also winter on inland lakes, reservoirs, and flood waters. Since first beginning to breed in the north of Scotland little more than a hundred years ago, the wigeon has now spread all over Scotland and into the English Border counties, and its nest of down and heather stems or grass may be found in such varied situations as hill lochs, moors, islands, and boggy mosses.

The little teal duck (14 in.), not much more than half the size of a mallard, could not be confused with any other duck except the garganey and possibly the wigeon. Though she is a sober-coloured, mottled-brown little duck with pale spotted underparts, a glinting metallic-green patch known as the speculum is usually prominent on her wings. The drake is greyer and, at close range, is distinguished by his curious brown and dark-green head-patterning and by vivid golden flanks. Further distinctions are their rocketing twisting flight and the bleating whistles and fluty piping of the drakes, the ducks doing no more than repeat a clear harsh *quad-quad*. Resident, passage migrant, and winter visitor, they are to be found in all parts of Britain, frequenting similar feeding and nesting habitats to those of the mallard, though as breeding duck they are rather scarce in the south of England and the Midlands; but they do not usually associate in the enormous flocks characteristic of mallard and wigeon.

The garganey (15 in.), another teal, is a rather uncommon summer resident, arriving in March and April, and a scarce spring migrant. It breeds mainly in east and south-east England in fens, marshes, and water meadows, where it nests in long grass or tussocks of rushes, and feeds on small fish and frogs and the usual vegetable diet. The duck somewhat resembles the teal duck, but in flight reveals a very dull speculum, while her throat is white instead of spotted. The mottled-brown drake, however, is distinguished by a prominent white stripe curving down from eye to nape and a pale-blue forewing; and his peculiar crackling call-note, resembling the noise of a wooden rattle, is also distinctive.

With the pochard (18 in.) we are introduced to the diving ducks—those, that is, which obtain their animal and vegetable food by diving to a depth of a few feet for periods rarely exceeding one minute and more commonly for only twenty or thirty seconds. Their

Garganey (drake).

Red-breasted merganser, sitting.

crest at the back of his head, which is very noticeable on a breezy day. In flight white underparts and a white stripe on the wing are distinctive. The duck is the counterpart of the drake, but sooty-brown with dirty-white underparts, and lacks the crest. The drake is rather silent, but the duck has a bass purring call. Both can only be confused with the scaup, which will be considered among the marine duck; for though tufted ducks may occasionally be seen on the coast in hard weather and on passage, they are, like pochards, essentially ducks of lakes and reservoirs, where they obtain their food by diving. In the breeding season they are to be found locally in most parts of Britain, though mainly in the coastal counties, nesting on islets in lakes and near the edge of small lochs.

Quite a different type of freshwater diving-duck is the goosander (26 in.), which, together with the red-breasted merganser and the smew, belongs to the family of saw-billed ducks. These have long and narrow, toothed and hooked beaks, suitable for the retention of the fish which they catch in underwater dives of up to two minutes' duration. The swift torpedo-shaped drake goosander is a very large white or cream-coloured duck with a dark-green head, a black back and a grey tail, and blood-red beak and legs. As its breeding haunts on rivers and lochs, where it nests in hollow trees or crevices in rocks, do not extend south of the Solway Firth, it is a winter visitor only to English inland lakes, rivers, and reservoirs. Though some mature drakes are to be seen among these small wintering flocks, the majority are the red-headed and maned ducks and immature birds, which are grey and white. All saw-bills are normally very silent, though during courtship both ducks and drakes utter harsh barks.

Superficially, the red-breasted merganser (23 in.) resembles the goosander. The drake merganser, however, has a thickly spotted rose-brown breast, a white collar and a notable crest. The two ducks are difficult to differentiate, the merganser's crest instead of mane being the best distinction; but as the

plumage pattern and colouring are also quite different from that of the surface-feeding ducks. The pochard is a characteristic duck of inland lakes, reservoirs, and large ponds, and also of estuaries in winter, when the numbers of residents are increased by visitors from abroad, and when flocks of several hundred or thousand are to be observed both on the coast and inland. As a breeding duck it occurs locally throughout Britain, though mainly in the eastern half, nesting in thick cover actually on or close to the water, using reeds or other material to raise the nest above the water level. The plump, heavily built grey drake has a copper-red head, black breast and tail-coverts, and white underparts; while the drab brown duck displays a similar, though obscured, pattern. Both are rather silent, though the duck's guttural croaking is often to be heard in her nesting haunts.

Though the tufted duck's (17 in.) plumage pattern is rather similar to the pochard's, the drake's colour scheme of black set off by snowy white flanks is distinctive, with the addition at close quarters of pale-blue bill and legs, a gleaming yellow eye, and a hanging or estuary-stake the cormorant has a peculiar habit of standing with spread wings "hung" out on either side, as if in the act of drying them. This habit distinguishes it from the smaller, slimmer shag (30 in.), for not one in ten thousand shags will come to land for this purpose, though they will quite commonly spread out their wings while swimming on the sea.

You can see cormorants on almost any stretch of the coast of Great Britain during the winter, though there are considerable sections on which it does not nest. On the water, where it swims very low, it spends most of its time diving for fish, mainly "flatties," usually with a jump right out of the water, submerging for half a minute or a minute. In March and April, however, cormorants resident in Britain—and few of the older birds emigrate—repair to rocky islands and cliffs to nest in colonies of up to a couple of hundred pairs. Large "drum" nests of seaweed or often heather stems are constructed only a foot or two distant from one another; and from being an almost mute bird during the winter, the cormorant now becomes a noisy croaker.

The shag also appears black or brownish at a distance, but the adults are in fact a dark metallic green without any white markings—though the immature may be pale brown—while during the early spring and summer the adult grows a prominent crest curving backward, quite distinct from the cormorant's hoary mane. Shags, sometimes in "droves" of hundreds, swim even lower in the water than cormorants, with thin "periscopic" necks sticking up similarly, diving continually and for generally longer periods than the latter. They are not so often seen on the wing as cormorants, but are then recognizable by a habit of continually jerking up their heads and by their quicker wing-beats. Moreover, unlike cormorants, they seldom fly higher than a foot or two above the waves. They are exclusively marine at all seasons, roosting in caves or on reefs and nesting only on rocky coasts, mainly in the west and north-east, to which they return as early as February or

Shag, on its nest of seaweed.

March. Though several individuals may be found nesting on a short stretch of cliff, they do so singly on ledges or in cavities, usually well down the face of the cliff or in some deep gully. From these dark retreats they bray and honk hideously, with flashing orange-mouthed beaks, when an intruder appears on the edge of the cliff above. Their nests are constructed of seaweed or heather stems, but the actual "drums" are flatter than those of the cormorant.

Though there are about a hundred thousand gannets (36 in.) breeding in nine large gannetries and one or two smaller ones on various islands around Britain, mainly in the west and north, the majority move out of British waters during the late autumn and early winter. Thus it is in the period February to October that you are most likely to see this great white sea bird with its six-foot spread of narrow black-tipped wings. Flying in rhythmically wing-beating and gliding files off all the coasts of Great Britain, usually at a considerable distance offshore, numbers will intermittently collect to fish, plunging from a height, one after another, in spectacular crash-dives, until the sea "boils" with the fountains of spray thrown up by hundreds of bird "torpedoes." Among the dazzling white adults you may see some blackish or pied younger birds, though the majority of these disperse south to Biscay and North African waters during their earlier years. At their breeding stations on flat rocky islands or the ledges of precipitous cliffs the gannets congregate in thousands, constructing huge "drum" nests, a foot or so apart, of seaweed, grass, campion, and various flotsam and jetsam. The nesting area soon becomes a white-

Fulmar gliding, seen from above.

washed landmark visible for miles, and is noisy the day long with its occupants' ceaseless *gurrah, gurrah, gurrah*—though away from its nesting station the gannet seldom utters a sound.

With one exception, the fulmar (18–19 in.), the various petrels and shearwaters are the most difficult of all the sea birds for the novice to distinguish when they are on the wing—quite apart from the fact that some of them are only offshore birds of passage, while those that breed visit their nesting grounds only at night. The fulmar, however, is a daytime bird and does not resemble any of its relatives. Indeed, in size and colouring (grey and white) it is much more like a gull; but its straight dark-grey wings are in marked contrast to a gull's "angled" and usually black-tipped wings; while its habit of perpetually sweeping down to and up from the sea on rigid wings, continually banking and heeling over, with only the merest flap, renders its flight quite different from any gull's. When it comes planing noiselessly up to the cliffs you will note also the large, round, white dove-like head, with its black eye and curious tubular nostrils, peculiar to petrels and shearwaters.

Although the fulmar is one of the few birds to be met with far out in the Atlantic, where it feeds mainly on tiny squids, fish and floating refuse, it is a curious fact that breeding fulmars are visiting their nesting cliffs as early as November and December. Yet the first eggs will not be laid until the following May and the young fulmars will not leave their nests until September. Seventy years ago the only British nesting station of the fulmar was St. Kilda. Since then their spread down both east and west coasts has been phenomenal, and they can now be seen on most stretches of coast where anything in the nature of a cliff or turfy headland is available, while in one or two places in north Britain colonies are even to be found on crags a few miles inland. Though the vast majority nest on cliffs in scattered colonies of hundreds or thousands, some are content to lay their single eggs on

Female peregrine falcon; the stricken bird in the background is a mallard drake.

Male kestrel on a fir branch, with female in background.

stone dykes and tumbledown buildings. From these strange places you will hear them cawing noisily—though at sea they seldom utter more than a soft crooning note—and if you approach to within a few feet of one it will gradually work itself up into a paroxysm and squirt a stream of yellowish or reddish oil at you. If it is a good marksman your clothes may be impregnated with a musk-like "perfume," but its strength varies greatly from one bird to another.

Of the remaining petrels and shearwaters the great and sooty shearwaters are birds of passage. Of these the easier to identify is the sooty (16 in.), which, though its breeding grounds lie in the southern hemisphere, regularly visits British waters in the months of August, September, and October. You may occasionally pick one up from the vantage point of cliff or headland—but more commonly from a boat a few miles offshore—and recognize it by its all-over sooty black colouring, as it glides low over the waves, continually tilting its narrow rigid wings to one side or the other, in the manner of all shearwaters.

The great shearwater's (17–18 in.) home is also in the southern hemisphere, its only known breeding station being Tristan da Cunha. Rather larger than the sooty, the great shearwater is tawny brown (blackish at a distance) with white underparts, and is incredibly agile—now hawking low over the water with short glides and slow wing-beats, in airy gnat-like flight with straight, slender pinions almost meeting over its back; now skating along the surface at speed, using its webbed feet as skis; now actually flying into a breaker and emerging with wings still open, to snap up jettisoned fish-guts under the very beaks of the gulls that accompany every fishing smack.

The appreciably smaller Manx shearwater (14 in.) is a summer resident, returning to its breeding colonies on islands off the west and north coasts of Britain in February and March; but it wanders far and wide from these, and both during the summer and also the migratory seasons may be seen off all

Manx shearwater, by its nesting-hole at night.

coasts, and be recognized by its contrasting plumage of black above and white below and typical shearwater flight. At its breeding grounds it nests in colonies, thousands strong, in burrows which it excavates itself, two or three feet deep; but as those birds incubating are visited by their mates only at night—normally on dark nights—little is to be seen of them; but a great deal is to be heard, both above and below ground, during the hours of darkness, for they utter the weirdest shrieks and sobbing cries, which might be rendered *chi-chicargo, chi-chicargo*—while their mates coo like pigeons in their burrows. During the day they may sometimes be seen fishing offshore for such small fish as sprats, herrings, and pilchards, and toward sunset large numbers flock together preparatory to coming ashore after dusk.

The tiny storm and fork-tailed petrels (8 in.) are also summer residents, returning in May and June to their nesting stations, which are mainly on islands off the west and north coasts; but being deep-sea feeders on the small creatures found near the surface, are seldom seen in coastal waters except during stormy weather. The storm-petrel might be described as the house-martin of the sea, for it is a sooty-black bird with a white rump and is only six inches in length, though it has long wings and a square tail. The fork-tailed petrel is somewhat larger and browner, but the forked tail is not very obvious. It has, however, an unmistakably bounding and erratic flight, whereas the storm-petrel has a fluttering flight and often patters over the waves on its webbed feet. Both are exclusively nocturnal at their breeding colonies, and, like the Manx shearwater, leave one in no doubt as to their presence; for the "stormy" purrs and hiccoughs for minutes together without a break from its nesting place in the chink of a stone dyke, under a boulder, or in a burrow excavated in soft soil; while the fork-tailed makes a staccato drumming when in flight and a crooning noise in its burrow in similar situations to the "stormy."

GREBES AND DIVERS

Grebes and divers—all exclusively aquatic birds—are easy enough to identify in summer plumage, but are often extremely difficult to differentiate in winter plumage. All except the red-necked grebe and the great northern diver breed in Great Britain. Much the most commonly distributed of the grebes is the little grebe (10–11 in.) or dabchick. Wherever there is water with a little cover there you may find a pair of these small brown grebes, and know them for grebes by their silky-white underparts and the almost total absence of any tail. Specifically they are further distinguished in breeding plumage by rich chestnut cheeks and throat. Some winter on their nesting pools, though others emigrate to reservoirs, estuaries, and sheltered sea bays.

At this latter season all grebes lose most of their distinctive head colouring and adornments, and it would be possible to confuse the little grebe in winter quarters with either the Slavonian (13 in.) or the black-necked grebes (12 in.), though these two are commoner in coastal waters. But whereas the little grebe is brown and white at all seasons, the other two appear glossy black and white. They are indistinguishable at a distance, but at close range the black-necked may usually be identified by its tip-tilted beak and the Slavonian by its prominent black cap, for the black on the black-necked's head extends

Little grebe, also known as the dabchick, sitting on its floating nest of weeds.

Black-necked grebe, a rare visitor which seldom nests in Britain.

right down on to the cheeks below the eye.

Both are rare breeding birds, though a number of pairs of Slavonian grebes have been nesting regularly on lochs in north Scotland; while the black-necked also nests regularly, sometimes in colonies a couple of hundred strong, on a few lakes and lochs in various parts of Britain and Ireland. In its breeding plumage the former has a copper-burnished neck and breast, but a black head and neck-frill, or tippet, which is adorned with copper horns of feathers projecting back from its eyes beyond its head; while the latter has a black neck, and its golden-brown "horns" fan out down its neck.

Though shy and skulking, the little grebe is a noisy bird, and you are not likely to be long in its haunts without hearing its explosive reeling whinny from the depths of a reed bed; or perhaps you may catch sight of its head peering out from under a bank, the rest of its body submerged. When undisturbed it dives with hardly a ripple for small fish and other animal and vegetable food. Its nest is a heap of water weeds built up above the surface of the water in the cover of reeds or under overhanging river-bank branches, and the incubating bird covers the eggs with weed when it leaves the nest.

In contrast to the little grebe, the Slavonian and black-necked tend to be rather silent in their breeding haunts, though they, too, utter whinnying laughing cries. Their nesting habits and food are akin to the little grebe's, though the black-necked mainly eats insects.

The great crested and red-necked grebes are much bigger birds, of duck size, with long necks and beaks. Although the great crested (19 in.) may be seen in estuaries and offshore during the winter, it is typically the grebe of reservoirs, meres and lakes in many parts of Britain, with a total breeding population of

Slavonian grebe (male), approaching nest; this grebe is now a well-established British breeder.

some fifteen hundred pairs. In winter it is a blackish-brown grebe with the customary silky-white underparts and small black ear-tufts. In summer the latter are much more prominent and, in addition, a large expanding chestnut tippet is grown. At this season it announces its presence by a loud booming *kraa-oo, kraa-oo.* Although there may be more than one pair on the nesting water, each stakes out a territory several acres in extent. The nest—the customary raised heap of weed—is usually placed among vegetation not very far from the edge of the mere or lake.

The red-necked grebe (17 in.) is a scarce, but regular, winter visitor from Scandinavia, mainly to coastal waters in the east of England. In some winters one may sail down upon a flock of a hundred or more diving and pattering over the waters of a sea bay. Experience is necessary to distinguish it with certainty from the great crested, though the yellow base to its bill is usually in noticeable contrast to the latter's pinkish beak. As it does not grow a tippet in the breeding season, the red-necked's head is likely to be "cleaner" than those of most great crested grebes, which usually retain enough of the tippet to give them a distinctly hooded, cobra-like appearance, and there may also be some summer red on the former's neck.

The three divers are also very confusing in winter plumage. Much the most widely distributed off all coasts at that season is the red-throated (21–23 in.). A larger and thicker-necked bird than the two big grebes, it is usually seen swimming some hundreds of yards offshore. At this range it appears a dark greyish-brown bird with white underparts, including its neck, and usually has its head and slender tilted beak inclined upwards halfway to the vertical. At closer range the white speckling on its mantle suffices to distinguish it.

Even at a distance it is often possible to make out the contrasting straight strong beak of the much less common black-throated diver (22–27 in.) and its darker mantle; and this diver has a habit of continually rising in the sea to flap its short greyish wings, with its dagger-shaped bill elevated vertically. Most, though not all, of the commoner and often numerous great northern divers (27–32 in.) are much larger in the body and heavier in the bill, and more extensively white than the average black-throated. The great northern is more often seen on the wing than the other two, with long, drooping, snow-white neck stretched out far beyond its long and narrow, quick-beating wings, which are set very far back on its almost tailless, torpedo-shaped body. Though they breed no nearer than Iceland, small herds of great northern divers may be seen off the north and west coasts of Britain in full breeding plumage in early

summer, resplendent with velvet-black heads and white-striped collars. On a calm day you will hear their yodelling, yaffle-like, *hoo-hoo-hoo*, seven times repeated, carrying far over the sea. In winter they wail and caw harshly.

Both red-throated and black-throated divers nest in Scotland, mainly in the west and north, and are distinguished at this season by, respectively, wine-red or purple-black patches on their throats. The black-throated is further distinguished by a collar of vertical white stripes on its black neck, and by the white bands on its black mantle, in contrast to the red-throated's plain mole-grey mantle. For its nesting haunts the former prefers a large loch with an islet in it, and may obtain its fish in its nesting loch, whereas the red-throated prefers a small loch or mere pool, nesting on its edge and flighting to larger lochs, or more generally to the sea, to fish.

The quacking *uck-uck-uck* of these divers, speeding like arrows across the sky above their nesting haunts with a powerful swishing of straight "flat" pinions, is a feature of summer on the desolate moors and "flows" of the north. They also utter a variety of mournful and whinnying cries; among the commoner of these being a hooting *ow-ow-oo* by the black-throat and a wailing *ayoo* and *ow-oo-ow, ow-*

Red-throated diver, commonest of the diver family.

Great northern diver in winter plumage.

oo-ow by the red-throated. As divers are unable to stand upright on their webbed feet they must perforce nest within a few feet of the water's edge, laboriously heaving themselves forward to the hollow or heap of moss and weeds on which their eggs have been laid. All three are master fishers, and may remain submerged for upwards of two or three minutes at a time.

PIGEONS

Pigeons are not usually thought of as sea birds; yet one, the rock-dove, is found only in the vicinity of sea cliffs, and a second, the stock-dove, also occurs in coastal habitats among others. The wild rock-dove (13 in.) is presumed to be the ancestor of all domestic pigeons, and even today numbers of the latter are continually reverting to the wild state, often nesting in cliffs. For that matter the hundreds of thousands of domestic pigeons, which are such a feature of the bird life of large towns, lead just as natural and wild an existence as town house-sparrows.

Observe a blue-rock homing-pigeon with two black wing-bars and a white rump, and there you have the prototype of a wild rock-dove. Take away the wing-bars and substitute a blue rump for the white one, and you have the stock-dove (13 in.)—always remembering that a little black shows on both wings and tail. Add a broad white wing-bar, a white neck-ring and several inches to the bird's length, and you have the wood-pigeon (16 in.) or ring-dove.

Picture a very small pigeon, a dove, with the blue-grey colouring replaced by tawny-brown on the mantle and lilac on the under-parts, with the addition of a rather long and graduated black tail with conspicuous white tips, and you have the turtle-dove (11 in.).

Wood-pigeon, stock-dove, and rock-dove are all residents in Great Britain. Numbers, often immense, of wood-pigeons, however, also come in from the Continent to winter, and at all seasons it is by far the commonest pigeon in most parts of Britain, often feeding in flocks of hundreds or thousands in beech woods and on fields of young corn. A heavily built bird with a small head, the wood-pigeon is distinguished on the wing by its powerful "clipping" flight and that conspicuous white wing-bar. During the nesting season—which, though normally in the period April to September, includes every month in the year —solitary pairs are to be found in a wide variety of habitats, from overgrown hedge-rows and trees to crags and town buildings. The nest is a small flimsy platform of twigs, and is sometimes placed on the top of an old nest belonging to another species of bird. In such situations the wood-pigeon's familiar cooing, "take two coos, boo-hoo," may be heard in every month of the year, though least commonly from November to January.

The stock-dove is not usually seen in flocks of more than a dozen or a score—though its feeding habits are similar to the wood-pigeon's—and it is much more local in its distribution. During the breeding season it may nest solitary or in small colonies, and is a hole-nester in such varied sites as hollow trees, rabbit burrows, sea cliffs, and inland crags. It does not coo so frequently as the wood-pigeon, nor very commonly in the autumn and winter, and its coo is a "bumpy" coughing *coo-wugh, coo-wugh.*

So many domestic pigeons take to breeding

wild in their ancestral homes in sea cliffs that it is probable that no pure wild stock is to be found in England and Wales, though you can watch what appear to be authentic rock-doves off the west coast and also Yorkshire. Even in the remotest islands of Scotland and Shetland wild and domestic stock are often to be seen feeding together on cornfields and pastures. However, when they have finished feeding, the present wild stock invariably return with swift and dashing flight to their roosting caves.

In the breeding season—as erratic as that of other pigeons—their nesting places are crannies in the cliffs, ledges in caverns, or niches under boulders on the beach. Like all pigeons they feed their young by regurgitating a milky fluid, and their cooing exactly resembles the tame pigeons.

The turtle-dove is a summer resident in Great Britain (and also a passage migrant), arriving from tropical Africa late in April and dispersing as far north as the Border, though numerous only in the south, east, and midlands. In these localities several pairs will nest in scattered colonies in open woodlands, parks, hawthorn plantations, or overgrown hedgerows; and all day long in sunny weather you may hear their purring crooning; and watch them mounting steeply up from the trees with slow flapping flight and then gliding

down again, white-tipped tails spread against the blue sky. The nest, like that of the wood-pigeon, is a very slight flat platform of twigs, sometimes lined with roots. To feed, the turtle-doves repair to open pastures, taking a little corn, but mainly the seeds of weeds.

WADERS I: CURLEWS, SANDPIPERS, AND OTHERS

Most waders have beaks and legs long in proportion to the size of their bodies, and admirably suited to the pursuit of mollusca, crustacea and marine worms and insects in their typical haunts, which are mudflats of coasts and estuaries, and the seashore, both sandy and rocky. Most, however, may also be seen in much smaller numbers at such inland habitats as sewage farms, marshes, and reservoirs with plenty of shore. On the coast the various species often flock together in thousands, especially at high water, when the tide covers all the mud and leaves only an occasional sandbank or reef exposed. They are all birds of swift flight and, at such hours, their vast flocks may be seen streaming over the flooded flats or the edge of the sea with the speed of an express train, twisting and turning with marvellous cohesion.

Although the months from September to May cover the great period for waders on the coast, when the hard core of winter visitors

Wood-pigeon, largest of the British wild pigeons.

Stock dove, bird of the open country.

is supplemented by others on passage and by breeding birds down from marsh and moor, there are always some waders, both breeding and non-breeding, to be seen on the more northerly coasts in every month of the year. These "perpetuals" include individuals of the following species: bar-tailed godwit, curlew, turnstone, knot, dunlin, purple sandpiper, sanderling, redshank, ringed plover, grey plover, and oyster-catcher; while on or very near the shore, especially in hard weather, there will also be found golden plover, lapwing, and common snipe.

With these fourteen species serving as stock types we can consider against their appropriate types those twenty-five less common visitors and rare wanderers to Great Britain. Numbers in both categories also breed with us in all types of country from sea level to mountain plateaux; but those that are regular breeders will be indicated thus: COMMON CURLEW.

The biggest and also one of the commonest

Black-tailed godwit.

waders on the shore is the greyish-brown COMMON CURLEW (19–25 in.). Its large curving bill, several inches in length, and very long legs, together with its husky *courr-lee, courr-lee*, distinguish it from all others except the smaller and darker WHIMBREL (18 in.). The latter, however, is an autumn and spring visitor only, when passing along the coasts of Britain to and from winter quarters in Africa and breeding grounds in northern Europe, though a few pairs also nest in Orkney and Shetland. As it is a much more confident bird than the curlew, one can usually approach it sufficiently closely to note its shorter and less curved beak and the salient buff-coloured stripe on the crown of its head; while its seven-syllabled silvery tittering cry is unmistakable. Constantly uttered on the wing, this musical whistling usually draws attention to a small flock of migrant whimbrels long before one ever picks them up with the binoculars.

If length of leg be a criterion of size, then the godwits are also big waders. Indeed, the black-tailed godwit (20 in.) stands almost as high on the legs as the curlew. But the godwit most commonly found on British coasts is the greyish-brown bar-tailed (18 in.), which is easily recognized by its very long and straight, though slightly upturned, beak. It is not a very vocal bird, its most commonly heard note being a sharp *pip-pep*, much resembling the black-tail's call.

While many bar-tails winter on Britain's coasts, often in flocks of hundreds or thousands, the black-tail is mainly a late summer and spring visitor in small flocks, especially to west- and south-coast estuaries and marshes. Until early in the nineteenth century it was a nesting bird of east-coast fens, and from time to time a pair still nests in southern and eastern England. In addition to its much longer shanks, which stretch far out beyond its black-banded white tail in flight, the black-tail is further distinguished from the bar-tail by the white stripes on its wings, by its very long neck, and generally by chestnut tinting on head and shoulders. Although the bar-tail

Male merlin (with wings outspread), with female and young of a few days old.

Common buzzards; the smaller figure in the background is an unusually dark variety.

Adult golden eagle with young bird in background.

Male sparrow-hawk, with old female in background seizing sparrow.

is also a burnished fiery orange in breeding plumage—it nests in northern Europe—comparatively few with any red on them are seen in Britain.

Another long-legged wader to be seen commonly on the shore is the REDSHANK (11 in.), which, however, is a much smaller bird than the godwits. Drab-brown in colouring, it is distinguished by the broad white bordering to the hinder edge of its wing, and by its orange-red legs, black-tipped orange-red beak, and pearly-white underparts. Like most of the sandpipers it has a habit of continually bowing on flexed shanks. It is also the noisiest of all the waders, breaking from plaintive *tew-phew-phew* into a frenzied shrieking on the first sign of any intruder. It seldom associates in flocks of more than a score or two of individuals, and is more often to be seen feeding solitary in a variety of situations from tidal pools on the sands and reefs to gutters on the mudflats, and on adjacent pastures and marsh streams.

Very much resembling the redshank—especially the immature redshank whose legs are plain orange—is the reeve, as the female of the ruff (11 in.) is known. There are no very obvious distinctions between reeve and redshank at rest, though the former shows a narrow white wing-stripe and a white patch on either side of the dark central portion of its tail in flight, in contrast to the redshank's black-barred tail; while its legs may vary in colour from orange to brown or green. It is, however, a very silent bird, though occasionally uttering a clear *knut-knut* or loud *screeoo*. The ruff is usually considerably bigger than the reeve, and some of those visiting Britain on passage are adorned with those remarkable multi-coloured ruffs and ear-tufts for which they are famous in their European breeding haunts. Although formerly a breeding bird of the fens, the ruff has nested in Britain only rarely in recent years, and those that now visit the country, regularly but in small numbers, do so mainly on spring and autumn passage. Though these visitors may frequent estuaries, they occur much more commonly

on fresh-water marshes and at sewage farms.

A less common autumn visitor from northern Europe to similar localities, mainly in the south and west, is the spotted redshank (12 in.). Although its plumage and colouring are not unlike the common redshank's, you are not likely to confuse the two, for it is a much darker and more stoutly built bird with a dark-coloured beak; and, being even shyer, is usually seen in flight, when its very bright orange-red shanks project farther beyond its tail, and a white "slit" up the lower part of its back is prominent. It is most easily identified, however, by its call-note, which it nearly always utters on taking wing—a clear throaty *chewvee, chewvee*, which cannot be confused with that of any other wader except the GREENSHANK (12 in.). The latter, however, uses this note mainly at its breeding grounds; its typical cry at other seasons being a clear *tew-tew-tewk*. Moreover, the greenshank is a very white and ashy-grey bird with a slightly up-tilted bill, and stands higher on its green legs than do the redshanks. Another shy wader, it is almost always solitary and is usually first observed towering to a height from its feeding place, where it dashes through a shallow pool or gutter in the mudflats, with head half under, chasing small fish.

The turnstone (9 in.) and its frequent companion, the much less numerous purple sand-

Sanderling in winter plumage.

121

piper (8 in.), are two waders specializing in reefs and rocky islets. When they frequent mudflats or sandy bays they are normally to be found on mussel-scaps or rocks, for they feed mainly on the insects and minute crustacea and mollusca that congregate in seaweed beds and under stones and in rock crevices. These, the turnstone—an Arctic nester—hunts in small flocks, with a good deal of pugnacious reeling chatter, by pushing over the weeds and stones with its bill; while a characteristic feeding ground of the often solitary purple sandpiper is in the rock-pipit's spray-misted haunts right out at the end of a reef.

Both are easy to recognize. The turnstone, which is a larger and more stoutly built bird than the ringed plover, is heavily mottled on the upperparts with purple-brown or rich tortoiseshell, with a black or brown breast-band

Greenshank at nest, often found near rocks.

and short thick orange legs set far back on its body. In flight this colouring breaks up into a unique dark-brown and white echeloned pattern.

The similarly sized purple sandpiper—whose nearest breeding haunts are in the Faeroes—is equally distinctive, the adult being the darkest of the sandpipers, for its mantle is purple-black laced with white. It has rather short dull-orange legs and bill and a white-rimmed black eye. It is further distinguished by its tameness, permitting the observer to approach to within a foot or two of it, and only calls when taking to the wing, uttering a grating trill or a soft sharp *tweet*.

The sandpipers are a numerous family, and their hosts congregate on the shores and mudflats from autumn to spring. With the exception of the "shanks" the largest of them is the knot (10 in.). An Arctic breeding species, the knot winters locally on the coasts of Britain in flocks, sometimes thousands strong, which often feed on the mudflats in dense grey "carpets." About the size of a redshank, but with much shorter green legs, it is a pale-grey and whitish wader with a small sharp head and beak, though some of those passing through in autumn and spring are dark grey on the back and pale orange beneath. It is rather a silent bird, and its call-notes usually take the form of a soft twittering, as the flocks perform their intricate communal evolutions on the wing.

Also pearl grey and white, very white in full winter plumage, but with boldly contrasting black at its shoulders and along the wing-edges, is the sanderling (8 in.), another Arctic breeding species, passage migrants of which may be tinted with buff or chestnut. It is a distinctly smaller bird than the knot, and has a sharp musical *swoo-eet* flight-note. It does not commonly associate in enormous flocks, but is usually seen in small "trips" of ten or twenty, which twinkle along the edge of the tide on short black legs on sandy shores, often in the company of other small waders.

Constant companion of the sanderling, and closely resembling it in size and plumage, is the most widely distributed and numerous of all the waders, the DUNLIN (7 in.), which flights in enormous flocks at high water. Passage dunlin are easily distinguished from sanderling by black blazons on their bellies, but in winter plumage these are reduced to a grey striping on the breast. At all seasons, however, the dunlin's greyish-brown mantle is much darker than the sanderling's, and, while a black rump is revealed in flight, its beak is longer, its call-note is an unmistakable whispered *tissee*, and it tends to feed farther up the shore from the tide and also more on mudflats, probing around and about in one place.

Another Arctic nester and a regular though uncommon passage visitor to the shores of Great Britain, mainly in the autumn, is the tiniest of the waders, the little stint (6 in.). It might be described as a diminutive dunlin (which it often accompanies), with a rounded head, short bill and white breast. When it takes wing, with a *sweet-tweet-tweet* alarm-note, it characteristically mounts higher than the other small shore waders.

It could be confused with the rare Temminck's stint (6 in.), which, though a north European bird, has attempted to nest in the central Highlands of Scotland. This, however, is a greyer bird with a greyish breast and white outer tail-feathers, a sharp spluttering flight-note and a habit of towering when flushed; and it is more likely to be seen at sewage farms and fresh marshes than on the shore.

Often associating with small flocks of dunlin and little stint on shore and mudflats, and sometimes inland, during the passage seasons, is the curlew-sandpiper (7 in.) from Asiatic Siberia. Superficially resembling a dunlin, its dark-edged white rump is distinctive when it rises into buoyant "flipping" flight with a soft *twee-twee*. Moreover, having longer legs, it appears bigger than a dunlin or sanderling, and in most individuals the bill is distinctly curved. (Some dunlin also have bills with slightly curved tips.)

Quite a different type of wader are the common, green and wood-sandpipers. These three

Turnstone (male).

usually occur singly on passage and not in the winter and are not commonly waders of the open shore and mudflat, but of marsh and sewage farm; though the common sandpiper also occurs regularly on rocky shores and in the creeks of estuaries. Though dunlin-sized birds, they are slimmer and stand higher on greenish legs than the small shore waders, and have a habit of continually bobbing up and down. Much the commonest of the three is the COMMON SANDPIPER (8 in.), which is brownish-grey with pure white underparts and

Turnstone (female).

a white wing-stripe. In contrast to the dashing flight of the shore waders, this sandpiper has an unmistakable hesitant fluttering flight, skimming low over the rocks or water. Its shrill *pee-pee-pee* is a very familiar sound in autumn and spring, especially at dusk.

Though the green sandpiper (9 in.) has nested once or twice in this country, it is primarily a not very common bird of passage from northern Europe, easily identified by its clear musical *toos-leep, toos-leep*, as it towers up with twisting flight from some marsh or sewage-farm pool or mudflat gutter—for it is a very shy bird. In flight it is immediately distinguished by its white rump, which contrasts with its blackish mantle and pearly white underparts, as in the case of the house-martin.

The wood-sandpiper (8 in.), which has also nested in Britain, is an uncommon migrant to similar localities from northern Europe. In flight it lacks the clean-cut contrasting black-and-white plumage of the green sandpiper, and the underside of its wing is greyish instead of blackish, as in the case of the latter; while at rest its mantle is generally much more speckled. It does not normally "tower" to the same extent, and its flight-note is shriller than the green sandpiper's.

To conclude the sandpipers we must mention a rare wanderer from Arctic America, the American pectoral sandpiper (7–8 in.),

Common sandpiper at nest, usually found not far from water.

Whimbrel approaching hatching eggs at its nest, a slight hollow in the rough grass.

which is intermediate in size between a dunlin and a reeve, with a characteristic black-and-brown striping on its mantle and a black-and-buff streaked gorget.

It is a curious fact that of the fifteen species of waders breeding regularly in Britain only two, both plovers, nest on the shore, and these not exclusively so. The remainder nest in a variety of inland habitats, from fields and bogs to the moors and mountain plateaux of the Scottish Highlands, in which region they are indeed extremely abundant.

The redshank occurs in most suitable marshy and water-meadow localities, both inland and on the coast, nesting in a tuft of long grasses, the tips of which are bent over to form a framework above the eggs. From April on its liquid *plleeder, plleeder, plleeder* and monotonous *plew-plew-plew* is to be heard, the day long, as the cock-bird rises and falls on rapidly vibrating wings above its nesting territory.

To see most British wading birds in their nesting haunts, however, we shall have to

Curlew, unmistakable with their curved bills, photographed at the edge of the tide.

travel progressively farther north. Though a few pairs of curlew, for example, nest on the heaths and commons of the southern counties, it is not until one reaches the Welsh Marches and the Peak District that they become a feature of grassy moors and bogs. There, all day long from March onwards, one hears their long-drawn-out bubbling trills (which may also be heard regularly on the shore in winter), preceded by a slow *whaw-up*, *whaw-up*, as the great birds mount steeply into the air and then make a long glide earthwards. The nesting pairs are, however, well scattered, half a mile or a mile apart, their nests being large hollows with a lining of grasses or heather stems.

The few pairs of whimbrel nesting on the moors and islands of the North Isles, from May onwards, also flight like the curlew above their nesting places with a very similar, though softer and more trilled, "skirling."

Though the common sandpiper nests locally in the west of England, it too is not common south of the hill country of Wales and the Peak, for it is to be found mainly on rocky hill-streams and stony tarns and lochs, arriving in these localities, which may lie above two thousand feet and exceptionally three thousand feet, in April or May. Although many nest on shingle banks in, or on the edge of, a river, a characteristic site is in the heather or grass a few yards above the stream. The grass-lined hollow is usually partially concealed by herbage; but the bird is extremely tame and gives its position away by flying round and round the intruder, or by bobbing about on boulders within arm's-length, piping incessantly its shrill lisping *psee-eep*.

For nesting dunlin it will be necessary to travel as far north as the Peak. Northward, from May onwards, you will hear their purring trilling *doo-doo-doo* as they circle and glide above their nesting territories on salt marshes by the sea, on moors, and on alpine pastures at a height of three thousand five hundred feet; but nowhere are they numerous. The nest is a cup hollowed out of a tuft of grass and lined with grasses or leaves, usually near water.

As for the greenshank, the central and northern Highlands of Scotland are its home; and there it may be found locally from March onwards in open, well-watered moorland and open glens. As the nesting birds will often fly several miles to feed in bogs and lochs—making a great to-do about this with their noisy *chuvee-chuvee-chuvee*—but are, in contrast, extremely silent and secretive in the vicinity of their nesting territory, the nest is difficult to locate; but the mere lined hollow is usually placed hard up against a boulder or pine stump or other prominent object. Occasional visitors to Britain include the Bonaparte's sandpiper (7 in.), which has a white band across its dark tail and a squeaky *jeet* flight-note; the broad-billed sandpiper (6–7 in.), with its dark striped mantle; the buff-

Curlew at its moorland nest, often built far from the coast.

Temminck's stint wading in a rock-pool.

breasted sandpiper (8 in.), which has buff-coloured underparts; and the yellowshank (10 in.), with its long bright yellow shanks, no light markings on wings, and a white tail.

WADERS II: SNIPE AND PLOVERS

Of the waders dealt with in this section only three—oyster-catcher, ringed plover, and grey plover—are characteristically shore birds. The largest, most conspicuous, and most numerously distributed of these is the pied OYSTER-CATCHER (17 in.). Brilliant red or orange beak and legs and black-and-white wings, together with its noisy piping *kleep*, render it unmistakable. Though sometimes congregating in enormous flocks on sands and mudflats, it may also be met with singly or in small parties on rocky shores, where it is much the commonest wader, being partial to shell-fish and able to lever the most obstinate limpet from the apparent security of its rock-hold.

Almost as big is the grey plover (11 in.), which is a winter visitor and passage migrant from the Arctic to sands and mudflats, where it usually occurs solitary, often in the company

of smaller waders, or in "trips" of a dozen or twenty. It is a fat bird with mottled dark-grey upperparts, black eye-patch, short black beak, rather long black legs, and the white underparts common to most waders. When it breaks into wild dashing flight, black "armpits" beneath its wings are revealed, together with a black bar across its snowy rump. Its sad, soft *phee-ee-ee* will attract your attention to its presence far out on shore or mudflat.

Very like it, but with upperparts mottled in dark yellow-brown and without the black "armpits," is the GOLDEN PLOVER (11 in.), of which there are two races, one breeding in Great Britain. Its plaintive *phee-ee* is not drawn-out like the grey plover's, and it has many other musical yodelling and twittering whistles. But though golden plover may be seen on the shore, especially in hard weather, they never stay there long and are essentially birds of farmland and fresh marshes, both on the coast and inland. In such localities they winter in sharp-winged silvery-bellied flocks of several hundred, usually in the company of still larger black-and-white, round-winged flocks of LAPWINGS (12 in.). The crested lapwing or peewit or green plover, with its black gorget and chestnut patch under the tail, and its *pee-er-wit* call-note, will be familiar to everyone. Like the golden plover it visits the shore and mudflats only briefly, though more frequently, and is mainly a bird of grazings and arable land.

A rather smaller and slimmer plover than either of these is the DOTTEREL (9 in.), which is a rare spring migrant in small "trips" to the hills and coast, on its way to northern Europe, though a few pairs nest on the highest mountains of Britain. Obviously a plover, it is an easy bird to recognize by the prominent white eye-stripes meeting at the back of its head, and by the rich chestnut of its breast, which is separated from its blackish-brown belly by a white band.

Quite different from any of these plover and one of the smaller waders is the RINGED PLOVER (7–8 in.), which is a very plump tawny-olive wader with black brow and cheeks, a

Heron and young of about two or three days old.

Gannet, also known as the Solan goose.

white collar, black breast-band and orange-yellow legs. In twisting flight its very long tapering grey wings show a white stripe. At all seasons it is mainly a bird of the seashore, in pairs or small "trips," feeding high up on the beach with sudden little runs and halts, and uttering a soft, characteristic *phooee* from time to time.

In 1938 a pair of the LITTLE RINGED PLOVER (6 in.), a western European wader not normally visiting the British Isles, nested at a Hertfordshire reservoir; and since 1944 several localities in south-east England have also been colonized. Rather smaller than its relative, the absence of the white wing-stripe distinguishes it.

The KENTISH PLOVER (6 in.) is also a very rare migrant and a decreasing, almost extinct breeding species on the shingle-beds of south-east England. Smaller than the ringed plover, its legs and beak are blackish, while the black markings on its head and breast are much fainter and less extensive.

The big STONE-CURLEW (16 in.), which somewhat resembles a small bustard, is almost exclusively an inland summer resident in Great Britain. A sandy-coloured bird, as large as a whimbrel, it has a large round head with very large yellow eyes, a short beak, and long yellow legs; while in flight its wings are conspicuously patterned black and white. Its flight-note is a weird shriek, not unlike, but higher-pitched than, the curlew's *cour-lee*.

Although the snipe family are not regular shore birds, they are sometimes to be found there, especially during the passage seasons and during spells of severe winter weather. All have very long tweezer-shaped beaks and rather long legs, conical heads with large eyes—they feed mainly at night—and a characteristically striped and barred brown-and-buff plumage. Of the three to be considered, only the COMMON SNIPE (10–11 in.) breeds in Great Britain, and it is the only one that is at all common at any season. Wherever there is damp ground there you are likely to find a snipe, and hear its sudden *etch-etch* as it zig-zags up from your approaching feet and

then towers to a height in swift erratic flight.

The jack-snipe (8–9 in.) is a winter visitor from Scandinavia and may be seen on the shore in October and November, its main arrival months, and in typical snipe country once it has settled in for the winter. It can usually be distinguished at a glance from the common snipe by its smaller size and shorter bill, by its habit of flying only a short distance on being flushed (when it tends to rise silently), without the other's zigzagging motion, and by its extreme solitariness; whereas common snipe often associate in small "wisps" at this season. At rest, it is further distinguished by the very bright ochre stripes on its mantle and by its head pattern, which lacks the pale-buff median stripe of the common snipe, but includes in its place two pale side stripes.

The great snipe (13–14 in.) is a rare autumn visitor from western Europe. It is hardly distinguishable from the common snipe in the field, though it usually rises silently when flushed, flies more directly, and is typically larger and darker.

Often accompanying the jack and common snipe on their autumn immigration is the

Dotterel, in its habitat on high, stony ground.

Female snipe sitting; the tip of its bill is flexible and can be used like tweezers.

rather snipe-like WOODCOCK (17 in.). It is, however, a much bigger and more heavily built bird than any snipe, and its wings are broad and rather rounded. When flushed it usually rises silently, with twisting flight and down-pointing bill. When settled in winter or summer quarters it is the only wading-bird favouring woods or bracken-clad hillsides, and is normally about only in twilight, flighting at dusk to its feeding grounds to probe for worms in ditches and boggy places. During the day it rests on dry ground in woods or other cover, and is extremely difficult to "pick up" against its background because of its beautifully marbled black, brown and buff plumage, and the unusual black transverse bars on its head.

It would be quite easy to mistake the two phalaropes in their pale grey and white winter plumage for stints or sanderling. The grey phalarope (8 in.), which is the larger, is an uncommon visitor from the Arctic, mainly to

130

Woodcock sitting; note the unusual size of its eye, a prominent characteristic.

offshore waters around the British coast (its feet are partially webbed), though it also occurs on pools, on mudflats, and at the usual wader haunts inland. Spinning in circles on a pool, picking up insects a few feet from one—for it is perfectly tame—the grey phalarope resembles a sanderling, except for a black smudge behind its eye, though its form is rather that of a diminutive black-headed gull.

Though breeding in very small numbers in Ireland, the Hebrides, Orkney and Shetland,

the RED-NECKED PHALAROPE (6 in.) is otherwise a very rare visitor to similar localities as the grey, from which it is distinguished in winter by its longer, thinner bill and the white streaks on its dark grey mantle.

Before going on to consider the nesting habits of these waders, there are two rare visitors to deal with, which do not resemble any so far mentioned. The least rare of these is the AVOCET (17 in.), which, though formerly nesting in Britain and regularly for the past

Stone-curlews changing task of incubating (above), *and* (below) *a newly hatched nestling.*

four years, is now mainly a scarce visitor from across the North Sea. A beautiful snowy-white whimbrel-sized wader with black markings, a long, slender, and uniquely up-curving bill, and long pale-blue legs, it could not be confused with any other wading bird on the shore. Nor could the BLACK-WINGED STILT (12 in.), which though a still rarer visitor from south-west Europe, has also been known to nest. Though also black-and-white and only slightly smaller than the avocet, the stilt possesses by far the longest legs proportionately of any wader; these are aptly described as red stilts.

Only the oyster-catcher and the ringed plover nest on the shore; but though the former nests commonly on many parts of the English coast and all round Scotland, it is also very numerous inland in Scotland, nest-

132

ing as much as seventy miles up the glens from the sea and often on grassy braes several hundred yards from the river. In such localities the noisy piping parties, with their rippling *kervee*, *kervee*, *kervee*, are as familiar a feature of spring, from March onward, as they are on the seashore. They are, however, characteristically the breeding birds of island and shore, scraping a hollow in the sand or shingle, or sometimes in the turf or thrift on top of the cliffs two or three hundred feet above the sea, usually lining the nest-hollow with small pebbles or shell fragments.

Though the vast majority of ringed plover nest on the shore, from March onward a few pairs nest inland on brecklands and river beaches, scraping a similar shell-lined hollow or sometimes cunningly hiding the "nest" in a tuft of marram grass. Hawking up and down the nesting beach, twisting and turning, the

A large gathering of oyster-catchers waiting for the turn of the tide.

cock utters an interminable *cadooee, cadooee, cadooee*.

The golden plover, on the other hand, nests inland on moors and on mountain "pastures" up to three thousand five hundred feet, returning to these territories in February or March. In its breeding plumage it is adorned with a ragged black breast and throat, and it is possible to identify birds of the northern race on passage in the spring by the more uniform blackness of these areas and by the greater extent of the yellowish-white eyestripe or line bordering them. The widely scattered pairs of breeding plover lay their eggs in slight hollows in short heather or in peat-hags, and the cocks circle high above uttering their mournful *tirr-phee-ew, tirr-phee-ew*.

Although you might possibly find a pair of

Little ringed plover (6 in.) which has bred in Britain in small numbers every year since 1944.

Ringed plover (7-8 in.), common nester on the seashore.

dotterel nesting on a Lakeland or Cheviot fell in May, you are more likely to do so on the Grampian and Cairngorm mountains of the central Highlands, though you will have to climb to over three thousand feet to do so. Though fearless, not all dotterel are as excessively tame as has been suggested. You may indeed experience considerable difficulty in locating the nest—which is a mere hollow in the stones and moss—especially as there may be only half a dozen pairs nesting in a mountain area covering fifty square miles or so.

Nor is the species a noisy one, its most prominent note being a slow melancholy *phwueep, phwueep, phwueep*. It is a peculiarity of the dotterel that the hen is larger and more brightly plumaged than the cock, and that the latter does most of the incubating and brooding.

The lapwing seldom nests above fifteen hundred feet, but breeds on grassland almost anywhere in Britain, scraping a hollow and lining it with grass stems. A number of pairs usually nest in the same field or marsh, and all day long and at night, too, when there is a moon, from February or March onwards, one hears the cock birds' wild crying—*wulloch-wooee, zoowee-zoowee, zoo-oo-wee*—and the musical swishing of their broad, "lapping" wings, as they flight and tumble with reckless abandon over their nesting territories.

The stone-curlew is a local nester only, from March onwards, on brecklands, stony fields, and chalk hills in East Anglia, the Home Counties, and southern England, its eggs being laid on the bare ground. A number of pairs nest in the same area, and "off-duty" birds associate together, becoming very noisy at dusk, wailing and whistling.

The common snipe is to be found wherever boggy or marshy situations are available, except in parts of southern England. In these places the humming sound made by their outer tail-feathers, as the circling snipe dive steeply down over their nesting territories, is as familiar a feature, from March onwards, as the lapwing's crying; and hardly less so the monotonous *chip-per, chip-per* from one

Kentish plover, probably no longer a British breeder.

perched on a fence stob or crouching beside its grass-lined nest hollow in a tussock or clump of rushes.

The woodcock nests almost exclusively in woods, mainly in coastal districts and hill country, and usually at the base of a tree in a mossy hollow lined with dead leaves. An extremely secretive bird, the presence of nesting woodcock would be overlooked in most cases, so tightly do they sit, were it not for the cocks' habit of "roding." This twilight flighting of theirs, from March onwards, takes them up and down a regular beat at tree-top height along the edge of their nesting wood or along a "ride." It is advertised by a bat-like *tzissik* note and also a very low-pitched croaking. Mention must also be made of the woodcock's habit of carrying its young between its thighs and, exceptionally, on its back for considerable distances.

Finally, the red-necked phalarope, now in their summer plumage of slaty-grey upperparts, with an orange patch at the side of the neck, and white throat and underparts, return late in May to their small colonies on marshy lochs and pools, using a grass-lined hollow not far from the water as nest; and as in the case of the dotterel, the duller-plumaged cock is responsible for incubation and the care of the young.

Other wading and crane-like birds sometimes seen in Great Britain include the following: the red-breasted snipe (12–13 in.), which resembles a small red godwit, and has a distinctive white patch on its dark back; the cream-coloured courser (9 in.), which resembles a small sandy golden plover with curved beak, and has a black-and-white napeband, mainly black wings, and long yellow legs; the pratincole (10 in.), which resembles the plover on the ground, but in flight is like a huge brown swallow, with deeply forked black-and-white tail; the little bustard (17 in.), which is stoutly built and sandy-coloured, with short beak and long, straight, thick legs. It is whitish in flight, with "whistling" wings. There is also the common crane (45 in.), which is large and has grey plumage and

Drake sheld-duck and young.

Mallard drake, with duck in background.

Tufted duck, with drake in foreground.

Drake pochard, with duck in background.

"bushy" tail. Its loud trumpeting cries distinguish it from herons and storks.

TERNS, GULLS, AND SKUAS

To state that gulls are medium-sized or large white sea-birds with grey or black backs may prove misleading. True, there may be gulls following your ship in mid-Atlantic; true, there are few stretches of Britain's coast where you will not find gulls, at any rate in winter, while every fishing port and village is noisy with their screaming and wailing. But it is equally true that there is no part of inland Britain, industrial areas included, in which you will not see one or more species of gull at one time or another; while in many parts of the country there are more gulls than rooks following the plough. Furthermore, thousands of gulls nest inland in a variety of situations from sewage farms to mountain tarns.

There are also many inland breeding colonies of terns, which may be described as small, sharp-winged, fork-tailed gulls with pale grey backs and black caps. They do not occur in winter; seldom soar or fly at a great height, as gulls do; and feed on small fish, which they obtain by diving from a height, whereas gulls never do this and are mainly scavengers.

The skuas, which are also summer residents or passage migrants, are exclusively seagoing outside the breeding season, though occasionally occurring inland on migration. Though of a size with gulls, their dusky brown or brown and white plumage enables them easily to be distinguished; as does also their method of obtaining food by hunting gulls and terns and forcing them to disgorge their last meal of fish.

Five of the terns are regular British breeding birds. Of these the biggest and most heavily built is the dazzling white Sandwich tern (16 in.), which is further distinguished by the shaggy nature of its black cap, and by its yellow-tipped black beak, black legs, not very forked tail, and harsh grating cry *krooeech, krooeech.*

The roseate tern (15 in.), which is rare in Britain, though less so in Ireland, and does not nest inland, also has a black bill with, however, a scarlet interior; but it is a smaller and much more slender bird than the Sandwich, with very long tail-streamers, bright coral-red legs, and a rosy flush on its breast. It must be noted, however, that some Sandwich also display this rosy flush. The roseate has the most distinctive calls of all the terns: a harsh cawing *caa-aa* and a ringing *chu-vee.* These identify it on the wing among hundreds of those two other similar-sized red-legged terns, the common (14 in.) and the Arctic (15 in.), whose most commonly heard cry is a strident, screaming *quee-arrr.*

These two, besides having red beaks and shorter tail-streamers, are duskier than either Sandwich or roseate. From each other they can best be differentiated at close range by the fact that the common has a black tip to its vermilion bill, while in summer the Arctic's lacks this tip and varies in colour from coral-red to puce. But these differences are not constant and, while the Arctic has longer tail-streamers, a darker breast, shorter legs, and one or two call-notes peculiar to it—notably a *pee-wee*—identification is often a matter for the specialist. However, very few pairs of

Courtship display of roseate terns.

Arctic breed in the southern half of England.

The little tern (9 in.) presents no difficulties, as it is much the smallest, and has a yellow bill with a black tip, yellow legs, a white forehead, and a quiet *whuit, whuit* call-note. It must be noted, however, that at midsummer, when they begin to moult, a whitish patch appears on the forehead of all these terns.

The remainder of the terns are visitors only, though one, the black tern (9 in.), nested on various east- and south-coast fens and marshes until the middle of last century, and has recently been recorded doing so in Sussex. Otherwise it is a not very common passage migrant from across the North Sea to coastal marshes and sewage farms inland; for this is an insect-feeding marsh tern, whereas all British breeding terns are marine fish-eaters. Its summer plumage is all slate-grey and black except for a white patch beneath the tail, and precludes confusion with any other tern; for the white-winged black tern (9 in.), which is a rare vagrant from southern Europe, has white shoulders and tail and red bill and legs when in its summer plumage.

Arctic tern, which breeds in the Arctic and winters in the Antarctic.

Sandwich tern removing egg-shell after the hatching of the first of its two eggs.

Terns are erratic in their nesting habits, nesting in large numbers in one place one year —they are all colony nesters—but perhaps completely deserting it for another locality the next year. The typical nesting places of the Sandwich tern are sand-spits or rocky islets and, less frequently, saltings and the gravelly shores of inland lakes. They begin to arrive in such haunts late in March, and several weeks later lay their eggs in hollows in the sand, sometimes bare, sometimes with a sparse lining of marram grass. There is a tendency for a score or so of nesting birds to cluster together, almost touching, around a clump of marram.

Common and Arctic terns, which arrive in April and May respectively, also nest in very dense colonies, which sometimes include thousands of individuals, in habitats and localities similar to the Sandwich. Individuals of both will mob an intruder, striking him on the head with their sharp beaks. Quite often the two species nest together, and probably interbreed in a few instances, as the roseate will do, when an odd bird of this species nests among the common terns in June.

The breeding stations of the little tern are exclusively coastal; and while they nest in small colonies, the individual pairs are usually well scattered up and down the length of the shore, where they nest in bare hollows on sand or fine shingle.

All the adult gulls are, with a little experience, relatively easy to differentiate. Of those with pale grey mantles the commonest inland at all seasons is the black-headed gull (15 in.), which is distinguished by a dark brown hood during the breeding season. This is lost during the winter, with the exception of a dark smudge or two on the face; but its dark red

139

Little tern, smallest of the British terns, on its nest, a hollow scooped in the sand.

beak and legs and the broad white border to the fore-edge of its rather sharp black-edged wings preclude confusion with any other gull. The immature birds have mottled brown mantles and a black bar across the white tail.

All other British breeding gulls have white heads, though in the winter the latter may be shaded by a certain amount of greyish or yellowish freckling. The only other gull with a dark hood is the little gull (11 in.), which is a regular, though scarce, visitor from eastern Europe. Smaller than the black-headed,

appearing half its size in flight, it also differs in having a black hood and no black tips to its wings, though their undersides are dark; while its flight is buoyant and tern-like. Most of those visiting the shores of Britain are immature and, like young kittiwakes, have black, slanting bars across their wings.

Much about the same size as the black-headed are the kittiwake and the common gull. The kittiwake (16 in.) is, however, almost exclusively a seagoing gull with the Atlantic for a playground, rarely coming inshore except when following fishing boats or during migration in stormy weather. It has the wildest and most buoyant flight of all the gulls, as it banks this way and that, cutting the waves with the black tips of its long, slender grey wings. All the other grey and also black-backed gulls display white "mirrors" on these black primary tips; and the absence of these distinguishes the kittiwake in flight from the common gull (16 in.). Moreover, the latter is a well-distributed gull of sandbank, estuary and inland pasture, only frequenting the open sea on migration. At close quarters there is a further distinction between the two in the colour of the legs, which are greenish in the common gull, but black-brown in the kitti-wake; while the immature kittiwake is distinguished by a black yoke across its neck and by those black bars slanting across its wings.

Much resembling the common gull, though a third as big again, is the herring-gull (22 in.), the most numerously distributed and noisiest

Immature Iceland gull, not, as its name suggests, a native of Iceland, though it winters there.

A familiar sight at sea: gulls on their constant search for food.

of all gulls on and off the shores, though not so common inland at any distance from the coast. Even in flight the herring-gull's heavy head and bill distinguish it from the common, while at close quarters its "angled" beak is seen to be yellow with a red spot and its long legs flesh-coloured.

Two other grey-backed gulls visit the coasts of Britain irregularly in small numbers during severe winters, more especially the northern coasts. These are the glaucous (26 in.) and Iceland gulls (21 in.) which breed in the Arctic. Both are distinguished by the very pale shade of grey on their mantles and by the absence of any black on their wings. Both vary considerably in size from one individual to another. The average glaucous is a very heavy-bodied and broad-winged gull, almost as large as the great black-backed gull; the average Iceland is of a size with a herring-gull. As those reaching British coasts are usually in immature plumage, mottled and streaked with sandy-coloured bars and flecks, identification is difficult to the inexperienced; but even in flight it is seldom that one cannot differentiate them by the relatively much smaller head and beak of the Iceland, which has the trim shape of a black-headed gull. Moreover, for every hundred seen only one will be an Iceland.

A still paler-plumaged gull, the ivory (19 in.), is pure white with black legs and of a size with the common gull. It is, however, an extremely rare wanderer from the Arctic, seldom occurring farther south than Orkney and Shetland.

Of the black-backed gulls, the lesser (21 in.) is a typical herring-gull, except for its grey-black mantle and bright yellow legs. It is mainly a summer resident, returning to its breeding stations from late February onwards. Individuals of the darker-mantled Scandinavian race, however, visit the coasts of Britain on passage and in winter.

The great black-backed gull (26 in.) is the giant of the family and as big as a grey goose, being further distinguished from the lesser by its intensely black mantle and pale pink legs.

In immature plumage, the grey and black-

Herring-gull, also called the Brixham-gull.

backed gulls are confusing, as they are all heavily striped and mottled to a greater or lesser degree above and below with black, grey and brown. Herring and lesser black-backed gulls, for example, can be only doubtfully differentiated, though the latter tends to be darker; while the great black-back is less uniformly dark and the common gull has a whitish tail with a black bar at its base.

Lesser black-backed gull by its inland nest.

All the gulls, except the kittiwake, nest inland as well as on the coast. Breeding colonies of the black-headed gull may include thousands of pairs, which return early in March to a variety of situations from islands and sandhills to marshes, bogs, and hill lochs. Loosely constructed nests of any available vegetation are built close to one another. Breeding colonies will not be overlooked, for the breeding birds keep up an incessant clangour of harsh cawing.

The common gull, which is almost exclusively a Scottish and Irish breeding gull, nests more commonly inland, in small colonies on lochs, moors and hills, than on grassy cliffs or islands offshore. It returns to these in March and, some weeks later, constructs a nest consisting of a platform of grasses or other material. Its colonies are not so incessantly noisy as those of other gulls, though intermittently their members break into a screeching *gee-yah*, *gee-yah*, *gee-yah*.

By contrast, the herring-gull nests inland only exceptionally, preferring grassy cliffs and islands. While breeding in colonies of many thousand pairs, these tend to be scattered in lesser groups along the cliffs or right round an island, and are often solitary. Their nests are the usual untidy litter of any available material. Though numbers of herring-gulls roost during the winter at some breeding stations, others return to these in February. From then onwards through the summer there is little quiet in their colonies, which ring to their incessant howling *gerwyer*, *gerwyer*, *gerwyer* and the antiphonal *quee, querwew; quee, quer-wew* of cock answering hen.

The lesser black-backed gull nests more commonly inland on lochs, moors, and bogs than the herring-gull, and in similar habitats on the coast; but it does not normally nest on steep cliff faces as the latter does, and its colonies are not so vast. Its very similar call-notes are rather deeper-toned than those of the herring-gull.

The great black-back is predominantly a coastal breeding species, though some nest on inland lochs and moors. On the coast colonies of great gulls display a preference for the summits of stacks and islets, while many nest solitary up and down the coast, constructing enormous nests of variable material. Their colonies—to which those that have not wintered return in March—never approach those of the other gulls in size, and few contain more than one hundred pairs. The deep-toned barking *aw-oo* and *uggha-uggha* of even a small colony is a most impressive sound.

Finally, the little kittiwakes nest exclusively on ledges and in niches on steep cliff faces and in gullies and caves, returning to their breeding colonies, which often include scores of thousands of individuals, from February onwards. Once settled in, their clamorous *wick-gewer*, *wick-gewer*, is never stilled the day long. Unlike the other gulls, the kittiwake constructs a well-shaped nest-cup of grass or other material, managing to fix this on to the most insignificant rock base.

Of the skuas, the great (24 in.) and Arctic (15 in.) are summer residents in the extreme north of Britain, and the pomatorhine (18 in.) and long-tailed (14 in.) rather uncommon passage migrants from the Arctic. The biggest of them is the great skua, or bonxie as it is known in its Shetland breeding stations, to which it returns early in April. A very heavy-bodied bird, almost as large as the great black-backed gull, the bonxie has an overall

Great skua at its nest.

Great crested grebe, carrying its newly hatched brood of young.

Pair of little grebes and young of about one day old.

Turtle-doves.

Wood-pigeon.

Stock-doves.

Rock-doves.

ruddy-brown plumage with a silvery patch on its broad wings. At close quarters the brown is seen to be streaked with buff and there are often white markings on the head.

The Arctic skua is a much smaller, dusky-brown, or brown-and-white bird with a markedly small head, very long wings, and projecting, spine-like, central tail-feathers. It is so sharply streamlined as to remind one at times of a giant swift.

The pomatorhine has the same variable colour-phases as the Arctic, but is bigger and more heavily built, while its projecting central tail-feathers are broad and twisted. In the very uncommon, greyer-backed, long-tailed skua these feathers project so far beyond the tail as to resemble thin pliant streamers.

There are only a few hundred pairs of great skuas nesting in Britain, and they do so on grassy islands, preferring hills on these where available. There, each pair takes possession of a mound or hillock, from which it can obtain a wide field of vision, laying its eggs some yards off the mound in a hollow of grasses and mosses. They are not very noisy birds, but from time to time a pair will raise their white-blazoned wings above their backs, throw up their heads and reiterate a *kee-yuk, kee-yuk*. When an intruder approaches the nesting territory one or both birds will take wing and launch a fierce attack, often striking him heavy blows on the head with their webbed feet. To procure food for their young they chase gannets and gulls, forcing them to disgorge fish: but for their own food they kill smaller sea-birds, such as kittiwakes and gulls, and suck the eggs of such birds as eider ducks, which unwisely nest among them.

The Arctic skua is a lesser pirate, robbing auks and terns of their small fish, killing an occasional small bird, and sucking eggs. It, too, mobs intruders, striking them with small stinging feet; and also performs curious antics, when its nest is approached, waving its wings and rocking about on its legs, hissing and screaming. It is a noisier bird than the bonxie, uttering a wild *ayer-yah, ayer-yah* and a ringing *yeh-yeh-wow*. It returns to its breed-

Arctic skua in flight.

ing grounds at the end of April and nests in small colonies in similar situations to the bonxie, though usually on lower ground, laying its eggs on only the slightest platform of grasses.

Also seen occasionally in Britain are the gull-billed tern (14 in.), which resembles the Sandwich tern, but has a shorter, thicker bill without the yellow tip, and its tail is less forked; the Caspian tern (20 in.), with its strong coral-red beak and long black legs; the sooty tern (14 in.), which has a white forehead and underparts; and Sabine's gull (18 in.), which has a dark grey hood and mantle, a forked tail and black-and-white wings.

AUKS

Auks are rather small, mainly black-and-white sea-birds, which spend the greater part of their time swimming and diving in offshore waters. They enter coastal waters only when "oiled" in stormy weather and during the breeding season, when they repair to rocky coasts and islands to nest. At that season they may be seen flying at a height of several hundred feet, when returning from their fishing ground to their nesting stations; but normally they fly only a few feet above the waves with a rapid whirring of their rather short wings.

All except the little auk (8 in.), which is a winter visitor from the Arctic, nest in Britain. The little auk is the smallest of the family, a squat little black-and-white bird, smaller than a thrush. Indeed, with its very short tilted beak and whirring flight it might well be mistaken for a small passerine bird, say a dipper. To see any quantity of little auks it is usually necessary to go a few miles offshore in a fishing boat, for they feed on small sea crabs and small creatures found near the surface and come into coastal waters only during stormy weather.

Though also black-and-white, the razorbill (16 in.) is twice the size of the little auk, with a pointed tail and a large, deep, curiously compressed beak crossed by a white line, with another white line from base of bill to eye. Despite the fact that they are also offshore auks, the earliest razorbills are returning to breeding waters before the end of December, though it will be a couple of months or so after that before they come ashore to inspect potential nesting sites in cracks in the cliffs or in burrows under boulders on most suitable coasts of Britain. Although one island or one stretch of cliff may contain several hundred or thousand pairs of razorbills they tend to be scattered.

Like most of the auks, razorbills are more or less silent at sea; but at their breeding stations they may be heard intermittently snarling harshly, as they shuffle about the top of a boulder on the whole length of their legs, or alight from sea with half a dozen small fish held crosswise in their beaks for the young one.

The guillemot (16 in.) is always distinguished from the razorbill by its thin pointed beak and brown instead of black upperparts; though the northern race of guillemots, which replace the southern in most parts of Scotland, may be almost black on the back. (In winter all auks have white throats and cheeks.) A small percentage of guillemots, increasing northwards, known as "bridled," are distinguished by a white ring round the eye, with a white line running back from it over the side of the head. The earliest breeding birds are returning to, and also sitting upon, their nesting ledges for an hour or two on calm days before the Old Year is out, though the first eggs will not be laid until May. Unlike the razorbills, they congregate in vast numbers on the steep faces of cliffs and the

Razorbills, which spend almost eight continuous months of the year at sea.

Black guillemots in summer plumage seen on a cliff ledge.

flat tops of stacks. A single cliff face may hold several thousand guillemots, with hundreds packed together as tight as they can squeeze on every ledge and platform, hard up against the cliff wall: sitting birds incubating their large eggs or brooding young on the bare rock, with their mates beside or behind them. They jostle and stab at one another incessantly, to the accompaniment of a continuous massed, almost organ-like, thunder of harsh cawing and a variety of other notes; and every new alighter with fish for the young stimulates a fresh crescendo of cawing. Unlike the razorbill, the parent guillemot brings up only a single fish at a time, which is held lengthways with its tail hanging out of the side of the bill.

The black guillemot (13 in.), or tystie as it is known in Shetland, is not a characteristic auk in either appearance or habit. Very few breed south of the Scottish Highlands, and to English coasts south of Northumberland it is a most uncommon visitor, though occurring in coastal waters more frequently than the other auks, when it does come south. Most of those seen south of their breeding stations are in winter plumage, with head and underparts mainly white and mantle laced and barred in blackish-grey and white. The summer plumage, however, is a uniform dark nigger-brown, except for a broad white patch on the wings, coral-red legs and a scarlet interior to the black beak. Both at sea and on land tysties utter very high-pitched piping notes, and are further distinguished by their habit of swimming in long files, with a score or two of individuals strung out in line. They return to their nesting waters in February, not landing, however, until late in April. Unlike the other auks, they nest in very small colonies, a few pairs nesting in crevices at the base of a cliff or under the boulders piled up above high-water mark at the head of a gully; while little groups may be seen standing *upright* on low cliffs, or crouched on boulders above their nesting holes, with small fish or crabs dangling from their bills.

The puffin (12 in.) is another black-and-white auk, smaller and tubbier than either razorbill or guillemot, and distinguished by its enormous conical, red, orange, and bluish-grey beak and its orange-red legs, on which it stands upright. After the breeding season, however, some of the brightly coloured adornments on the beak are shed, and the latter is reduced in size and becomes a coral-brown in colour. Unlike the other auks, puffins do not return to nesting waters from their Atlantic wanderings until March. Their colonies, which may number scores or even hundreds of thousands of individuals, are mainly restricted to grassy cliff sidings and

Common guillemots, including one of the "bridled" variety with its characteristic eye marking.

small islands on the west and north coasts of Britain. Such habitats are pitted with their burrows, though a few also nest in cliff crevices.

Though puffins may often be seen industriously pulling up grasses, few of them ever find their way down to the nest chamber two or three feet underground; and the most characteristic view of a puffinry is of thousands of comical little sea-parrots standing outside their burrows or padding bashfully backwards and forwards, while others are continually alighting with rows of tiny silver fish, held crosswise and head to tail in those powerful beaks. Unlike the other auks, the puffin is a very silent bird, and one seldom hears more than a brief sepulchral caw from beneath one's feet.

RAILS

With the rails we return inland, though coots often visit estuaries in hard weather, and both water-rails and corn-crakes have a habit of turning up on migration in such unlikely places as sub-oceanic islands and lighthouses. With the exception of the corn-crake or land-rail all are marsh or water dwellers, and the true crakes and rails are extremely secretive and inconspicuously plumaged birds, which would be almost wholly overlooked were it not for their extraordinary harsh or squealing cries.

Only one of them, the water-rail (11 in.), is resident, frequenting many watery places with plenty of cover in England, though not so commonly in Scotland. It stays mainly in the cover of reed beds and other vegetation, and one's occasional glimpses of it are of one fluttering into the nearest reed bed with legs dangling down; or of a very thin brownish bird, with smooth grey underparts, blue and white flanks and jerky tail—cocked up to reveal yellowish-white under-feathers—pacing gingerly on long legs over the mud, pecking at larvae or roots with its long pinkish-red beak. (It is the only rail with a long beak.) It is much more likely, however, that you will hear only its agonized groans and squeals. If

you are familiar with all the notes of moorhen and dabchick, then any strange cacophony from a reed bed is almost certain to originate from a water-rail. Its nest of dead reed leaves is hidden in the densest vegetation.

Another marsh rail, though an exceedingly rare nester and also passage migrant, is the spotted crake (9 in.). In general habits and appearance it resembles the water-rail, though it is a smaller bird with a short beak and a marked white speckling on its upperparts. Its ticking call-note is heard mainly from late evening onwards through the night. Its nest differs from the water-rail's in being lined with grasses, and is usually placed on a tussock of sedge or weed.

The little crake (7–8 in.) is also an extremely rare marsh bird and does not breed in Britain. It is very like the spotted crake, but may be recognized by its small size.

The corn-crake (10–11 in.) might be described as a large spotted crake, with buff-coloured plumage stained with reddish-brown: but as it is very rarely seen and inhabits a different type of country to any of the other rails, plumage distinctions are not important. Formerly a common summer resident of meadows and grasslands in all parts of Britain, from April onwards, the corn-crake is now numerous only in the extreme west and north of Scotland. To hear many *crek*-ing on summer nights, from the open strips of corn and potatoes or from the flats of wild hay, you will have to go to the Hebrides or Orkney Islands, or west Ireland. This monotonous rasping note sounds like a stick drawn across the teeth of a comb, a crunching *pank-pank*. Always skulking in thick vegetation, feeding mainly on insects, the corn-crake fashions a thick platform of grasses for a nest in a bed of nettles or flags or brambles.

It would be possible to mistake one of the marsh rails for an immature moorhen, but the adult moorhen (13 in.) is unmistakable in its rusty-black plumage, set off by red face-shield and yellow beak and white flank stripes; while its tail is continually cocked up,

Water-rail approaching its nest, characteristically situated in a marsh.

revealing white under-feathers on either side of central black feathers. When it swims, the bird jerks its head backwards and forwards; while, when walking about the grass, often at some distance from pond or pool, it does so with a high-stepping jaunty action. It runs swiftly to water with lowered head on the approach of an intruder, often breaking into clumsy flight with legs dangling. The moorhen is the most commonly distributed fresh-water bird in Britain, and wherever there is the smallest pond, from London parks to the Shetland Isles, there you may expect to find one or more pairs of water-hens; while in winter a score or more may flock together on some large pond or sewage farm, often roost-ing in adjacent bushes and thorn trees. Though usually rather a shy species, it does not stay long in cover after an alarm, and soon comes out to resume its search for food, which comprises a wide variety of vegetable and animal matter. Even when in cover its loud explosive croaking is heard intermittently; while on summer nights, when it is often on the wing, its *kek-kek* often puzzles the night wanderer. Its large nest-heap of dead water-weeds is usually placed at the edge of the water, though sometimes among overhanging branches; while occasionally a nest of grasses will be constructed in a tuft some yards from the water's edge, or in a hedge or tree hun-dreds of yards from the nearest pond.

Often inhabiting the same stretch of water as the moorhen is the coot (15 in.), which, however, prefers larger ponds, lakes, and reservoirs and is usually seen in numbers, winter flocks including several hundred individuals. A much bigger and heavier bird than the moorhen, the coot's all-black plumage is relieved only by its large white face-shield and bill. The grey-brown juvenile, however, lacks this shield. Not such a noisy bird as other rails, its most commonly heard note resembles the sound of a cork being withdrawn from a bottle. It is more of a vegetable feeder than the moorhen, and flocks may often be seen grazing on pastures near water. Its large nest of dead water-weeds is usually placed among the reeds and built up well above the water level.

GAME-BIRDS

Though all are game-birds, there is no single descriptive factor covering grouse, pheasants and partridges which would enable you to say of any one you saw in the field—that is a game-bird! Nor have they a common habitat, for their various kinds are to be found in such widely differing country as shooting coverts, marshy places or open plains, pine forests or

Corn-crake, or land-rail, sitting; it is now numerous only in extreme north and west Scotland.

moors, or the summits of the highest mountains in Britain. There are very few country people, however, who do not know a pheasant or a partridge when they see or hear one, and they are the typical game-birds of England, just as the red grouse is of Scotland.

The long-tailed pheasants (cock 30–35 in., hen 21–25 in.) hanging from poulterers' hooks must also be well known to every city dweller, and we need not linger over details of their plumage, except to note that those with red and green or purple heads, and usually a white neck-ring, are the cocks; the hens being a plain-coloured and less coppery brown. Although the pheasant was introduced into Great Britain at least nine hundred years ago, its status has always been mainly artificial, and when left to fend for itself it survives only in small numbers. Under such conditions it is noticeable that these wild pheasants, both in England and Scotland, retreat to those jungly swampy places which most resemble the oriental habitats of their ancestors. Where preserved, however, the pheasant is the characteristic game-bird of covert, hedgerow, arable fields and parklands—feeding on a variety of animal and vegetable foods—and its explosive crowing "jarr" and the hollow boom of its wings are features of evening in England. Most pheasants in Great Britain are polygamous, the hens scraping hollows in thick cover for their eggs.

Of the two partridges, the red-legged, or French (13–14 in.), is also an introduced species of less than two hundred years' standing, and does not occur in any numbers north of a line from Yorkshire to Somerset, being local in all districts. Its habitats and food— almost wholly vegetable—are similar to those of the common partridge, though it displays a special preference for sandy heaths, saltings and chalk downs. Though slightly larger than the common partridge it is by no means easy to differentiate between the two at a distance, though the red-leg runs more and flies less. At closer range, however, the latter is immediately distinguished by its black-bordered white cheeks and throat, blood-red bill and

legs, and the black, white and chestnut barring on its flanks. Its voice is also quite different, being a higher-pitched and throatier clucking than the common partridge's. Its nest resembles that of the latter, being a hollow in the cover of hedgerow or bush, grass or crops.

The common partridge (12 in.) is a tubby, grey and sandy-coloured bird, with a vivid orange-brown head and a dark chestnut horseshoe blazoned on its lower breast. It runs very swiftly in an upright posture and flies strongly with noisily whirring rounded wings, skimming low over hedges and farm buildings, spontaneously altering height and direction without apparent effort. Outside the breeding season partridges are invariably seen in small coveys, roosting at night together in open fields in these family groups; and their icy jarring *ker-wit, ker-wit* at dusk and in the early morning is a very familiar sound in agricultural country, and also in such land as sandy links, heaths, moors and hillsides throughout most of Britain.

Both in form and in flight the quail (7 in.) might be described as a tiny buff-coloured partridge, being only half the size of the latter: but it is seldom seen, for it is very reluctant to take wing from its retreat in the tussock grass or, in autumn, from the root fields in which it shelters while on migration from Europe to North Africa. Moreover, both as migrant and as a summer resident, arriving in May and June, it is now very scarce, nesting more frequently in crops, pastures and commons in the southern half of England than elsewhere. Where present it draws attention to itself by the continual repetition, day and night, of its unmistakable liquid call-note, long translated by country folk as *wet-mi-lips*.

Although one does not associate the Twelfth with English sport, there are in fact considerable numbers of red grouse (cock 15 in., hen 13 in.) on the moors of the Peak and Yorkshire, and of course in the Welsh hills, and a few in Devon and Somerset; and this is also true, to a much lesser extent, of the black grouse. Predominantly, however, the red grouse is the game-bird of Scottish moors.

Female woodcock and young, with male in background.

Pair of common sandpipers and young at the nest.

Pair of dunlin in breeding plumage, with young in background.

Ringed plover and young by a clump of sea-pea.

Since its staple food is heather, and in lesser quantities the berries of such creeping moor plants as crowberry and bilberry, the red grouse is not usually found off the moors: though during heavy snowstorms or prolonged frost extensive local migrations take place from hills or exposed moors to more sheltered moors. Outside the breeding season the grouse collect in small packs, and one's characteristic view of them then is likely to be of a bunch of heavy, dark, round-winged birds whirring down-wind at a great speed, "jinking" recklessly from side to side, before whirling over the brow of the moor. During the nesting season a grouse moor is a noisy place, especially in the early morning, and on all sides one hears the cackling *go-back, go-back, go-back* of excited cock grouse leaping into the air. Under such conditions one can watch them at one's leisure and admire their copper-brown plumage, set off by white-feathered legs and by large red wattles above the eye—much reduced in size in the hens. The latter scrape hollows in the heather or in tussocks of sedge for their eggs, with a few wisps of dead grass, moss or heather for nest.

At a distance it is quite easy to mistake a greyhen—as the female of the black-cock or black grouse (cock 21 in., hen 16 in.) is known—for a red grouse. It is not a mistake that should normally be made, however, for whereas grouse usually fly only a few feet above the heather, black-cock commonly fly at a height of some hundreds of feet on a straight course from one pine planting to another, in contrast to the red grouse's curving and erratic course.

Moreover, they fly with swift regular wing-beats, varied by intermittent brief glides; in contrast to the red grouse's noisy whirring action. Nor is the black-cock a regular inhabitant of the moors; though one or two, usually greyhens, may sometimes be seen feeding on the open moor at some distance from their home wood in the late summer, while local migrations of packs of a score or more occur in hard weather. Thus, opportunities for confusing the two species are infrequent. Actually, the greyhen is a greyer bird than the red grouse, with a wavy white wing-stripe, forked tail and unfeathered legs.

The black-cock himself is quite unmistakable, being a glossy blue-black grouse with dark-red "scimitars" over his eyes and prominent white markings on his wings and the curls of his unique lyre-shaped tail. Moreover, unlike red grouse, black-cock rise silently and call only when perched in the upper branches of the trees in their plantations of pine, larch, or birch scrub—for their staple foods are the buds and shoots of trees—or when at their *leks*. The latter are grassy swards in or on the edge of the plantations, which numbers of black-cock and greyhens visit at various times of the day during the breeding season, but especially in the early morning. At these *leks* the black-cock display and fight, to the accompaniment of a variety of call-notes, of which the most commonly heard, both at the *leks* and from solitary birds perched in trees, is a musical dove-like warbling *roo-kroo*. They are polygamous, the greyhens laying their eggs in bare hollows in the grass or heather.

Not unlike the greyhen—though more resembling a hen pheasant in her white-speckled, dull gold plumage with a tawny patch on her breast and a copper-edged tail—is the hen capercaillie (cock 34 in., hen

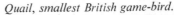

Quail, smallest British game-bird.

153

24 in.). The fact that she is a third bigger than the greyhen, as large as a goose indeed, is not always apparent in the jungly coniferous woods of the central Highlands which the two species share: for both are very shy birds, and the most one often sees of either is just a glimpse of a heavy greyish-brown bird hurtling through the trees after a muffled crashing in the undergrowth. Capercaillie spend much of their time on the ground, where the hen nests in thick cover usually at the base of a tree, though they also perch high up in the trees, feeding on their buds and needles. Once out of the woods they fly at a considerable height above the trees and may glide for a mile or more right across a glen from wood to wood. Their huge size is then apparent, and the cock is always unmistakable—a great grey, rather cormorant-like bird with a swollen head and light yellow beak, a metallic dark-green patch on his breast, a grey back and an enormous black tail.

As a native of Britain, the caper became extinct about 1760. It was re-introduced, however, some eighty years later, and is now to be found in small numbers in many parts of the Highlands, especially on the wooded slopes of glens. Its numbers, however, do not appear to be sufficient to encourage the formation of those display groups normal on the Continent: so that one may live for years in capercaillie haunts in Scotland and never hear a

Pheasant, a bird probably introduced into western Europe in Roman times.

Red-legged, or French partridge; its plumage is more striking than that of the common species.

sound from the cock capers, which are very silent birds away from their *leks.*

To see the ptarmigan (13–14 in.) we must go up out of the grouse country to the treeless stony barrens above two thousand feet, though occasionally one may come upon a pack of these little white grouse on the floor of some wild glen in the heart of the mountains at a height of less than fifteen hundred feet. But the high tops and high corries are the ptarmigans' home in the Scottish Highlands; and in these high places they are to be found, day in, day out, at all seasons of the year: for even when all the tops are buried beneath snow the ptarmigan are still able to burrow down through the snow to the berry plants which are their staple food. Although the cock's mantle and breast are blackish-grey in the breeding season and the hen's dull gold and black, their black-tipped white wings and their small size make them easily distinguishable at all seasons; as are also their curious staccato crackling, croaking, and belching call-notes. The hen lays her eggs in a scrape on the open moss or berry plants, and after the young hatch the family remain together until the autumn, when numbers may band together into packs, several score strong.

Migration and movement of birds

THERE are references to bird migration in ancient Chinese poems and in Aristotle as well as in the Old Testament. But as late as the time of Gilbert White, the naturalist of Selborne, less than two centuries ago, many people believed that some birds hibernated for the winter—and that theory is not quite dead even now.

The fact is that the progress of migration, on an impressive scale, is rarely observed. And yet vast movements take place. In the spring more than fifty bird species, involving countless individuals, come to Britain to nest and others pass through on the way to their breeding grounds in North Europe and the Arctic. In the autumn there are big southward movements. The swallows, cuckoos, warblers, and other summer visitors leave to spend the winter in South Europe and Africa. But many other birds, of over eighty species, arrive in Britain from North and East Europe and from Greenland and Iceland; some of these pass on south, while others stay for the winter.

We know of these movements from the changes we can observe in the bird population. The first sign that the summer visitors are on their way back may be when we hear the cuckoo calling in spring, and later notice that the swallows and the warblers have returned to their old haunts. In the autumn we know that the return migration has begun when the swallows pack together on the telegraph wires and the shores and estuaries become crowded with waders. The evidence of movement is plain enough, but we may see little or nothing of the coming or the going.

One reason for this is that migration does not take place in a sudden rush. It is spread over a number of months, with some species coming early and others later. And a very great deal of it takes place by night.

Some species, including swallows, swifts, and martins, and some of the crows and finches, do migrate by day, but they normally travel singly or in small groups rather than in large flocks. Mass movements, by day or by night, are exceptional and occur only after gales or in fog, when a number of separate flights may get bunched together. Moreover, a good deal of migration, especially inland, goes unnoticed because of the difficulty in distinguishing between migratory and purely local movements.

Nevertheless, and especially in the last fifty years, an enormous amount of information has been collected on the migrations and movements of British birds. Much of what is already known has come from people who have made careful notes of the dates on which they have first seen the summer migrants, and more from the detailed observations of such men as Gätke, on Heligoland, and Eagle Clarke, at the islands and lighthouses around Britain, and more recently from the bird observatories which have been set up on islands and headlands.

Many of the hard facts of migration have been discovered as a result of the marking of birds with light aluminium rings and their subsequent recovery, sometimes thousands of miles away. The ringing method has provided much information which could not

Autumn migrants: house-martins on a roof-top.

have been obtained in any other way. It is known, for example, that British-bred kittiwakes migrate right across the Atlantic to Newfoundland and that swallows nesting in Great Britain spend the winter in South Africa. It has also been proved that summer migrants frequently return to the nesting locality of the previous year, sometimes even using the same nest for several years in succession; there is also a growing amount of evidence which suggests that individual migrants may return to the same part of their winter quarters, as well as to their birthplace.

Migration is a good deal more complex than was at first imagined: although the peak periods are in the spring and autumn there is scarcely any time of the year when migration, of one sort or another, is not taking place. Most birds are subject to movements of a more or less migratory nature and there are very few, if any, species in Britain which are entirely sedentary. Even the red grouse, the only exclusively British species, often descends in the winter from the upland moors, where it breeds, to the more sheltered valleys. There are other local movements, such as those of the curlews and golden plover which spend the summer on the moors and the winter on the marshes and shore. Finches and tits, after nesting, band together in flocks and roam the countryside in search of food. Some sea-birds disperse for great distances without

Golden plover in brilliant summer plumage at its moorland nest.

Kittiwakes, which nest on the coast, mainly in the west of Britain.

appearing to travel in any particular direction. In the breeding season they are concentrated in vast colonies, but afterwards they scatter over the oceans.

But true migration is much more than dispersal; it is the definite and regular movement of an entire bird population, or the greater part of it, from one area to another, a movement to and from the nesting territory and the winter feeding territory. For some species these areas are quite separate, and even, as for the swallow and Arctic tern, in different hemispheres. For other species the winter and summer range overlaps; starlings, for instance, are largely sedentary in Great Britain, but on the Continent they are migratory, and after the breeding season the numbers of residents are swollen by the very large flocks which travel from the Continent and spend the winter in Britain.

Even among species commonly thought of as resident some individuals do migrate.

Indeed, birds from the same brood may behave differently, some of the young migrating out of the country and others staying around their birthplace. Partial migration is well shown by an analysis made by David Lack of the recoveries of birds ringed as nestlings. Song-thrushes and lapwings are examples of partial migrants, and in both these species some of the migrating birds go west to Ireland, while others go south to France and Spain. The difference in behaviour seems to be related to age and sex, for among the juveniles and females there is a greater tendency to migrate south than among the adult males.

Although quite a lot is known, by direct observation and from the results of ringing, of the kind of movements made by birds, of their destinations and of the routes they take, there are many problems which remain unsolved.

It is unlikely that we shall ever be certain

how migration originated. Nor is it easy to say why birds migrate. The advantage to a species must be very great, for it is often an expensive process in which countless lives are lost. There can be little doubt that the urge to migrate is part of the inherent rhythm of a bird's life (just as nest building is) and it is closely associated with the rhythm of the seasons.

Climate, and especially the effect of climate on the food supply, is obviously an important factor. Migration is most highly developed among insect-eating birds, and for them vast areas of the northern hemisphere are uninhabitable in the winter. But in the summer these areas become highly desirable breeding places, with an abundant food supply and long hours of daylight in which to feed the insatiable young.

But cold, or the difficulty of obtaining food, is not the immediate stimulus to the autumn migration. Many birds leave long before the approach of winter—in Britain the swifts begin to move away in July. The nature of the immediate stimulus is not yet clearly understood. Experiments have proved that changes in the length of daylight, and in a bird's activity, have a direct effect on the development of the sexual organs and through that on the urge to migrate. But the exact

Stonechat, a partial migrant.

nature of the relationship is still in doubt and there are anomalies which need to be explained.

Another complication is that some species differ in their migratory behaviour although they are very closely related in other ways. Eleven out of the twelve warblers which nest in Great Britain migrate, but one, the Dartford warbler, is an all-the-year-round resident. Again, stonechats and whinchats are similar in many ways, but the whinchat winters in tropical Africa and only flies to Britain to breed, while stonechats are resident, or at any rate only partially migratory. It is perhaps significant that both Dartford warblers and stonechats suffer severely in hard winters.

The problem of orientation, of how a bird finds its way from one place to another, is the most intriguing of all the unsolved mysteries of migration. Despite many theories, and many ingenious experiments, no solution has yet been reached which admits all the facts.

The "homing instinct" of many wild birds is very much better developed than it is in racing pigeons, which have to be carefully trained over gradually increased distances, normally all in one direction from the loft. With most migrants there can be no question of being taught the way. While it is true that some young birds travel with their parents, in family parties, in many species the young leave first and have to find the way by themselves. Again, young cuckoos may never see their parents and do not start their migration until some weeks after the adult cuckoos have left.

One of the oldest theories was that migrants follow definite routes, along coastlines and up river valleys, and there is no doubt that such routes are used where they lead generally in the right direction. But it is now accepted that birds often migrate on a broad front rather than along restricted routes. Moreover, some birds have no difficulty in crossing vast tracts of ocean; a striking example is the Pacific golden plover, which breeds in Alaska and winters in Hawaii, involving a journey over two thousand miles of open sea. The most

Lapwing and brood of young.

Golden plovers in winter plumage.

Oyster-catchers in summer plumage (front) and winter plumage (behind).

Pair of storm-petrels and young of a few days old.

interesting aspect of this flight, and it applies to other migrations, is that there must be compensation for the lateral drift caused by winds. With so small a destination the slightest deviation would mean disaster, and yet this amazing feat of navigation is regularly performed.

There have been many experiments on the "homing instinct" of wild birds. In a series of experiments with shearwaters from the Welsh island of Skokholm birds were taken from their nests and released in areas quite unknown to them. Shearwaters returned from up to 930 miles away and other species have got back from even greater distances. Some of the birds have had magnets attached to them, to negative the effect of the earth's field, as it has been suggested that magnetic sensibility was a possible explanation of homing. They arrived back just the same.

There is very little evidence of the speed at which individual birds travel when on migration. Ringing cannot help here; there are a very few instances of migrating birds being ringed and recovered many miles to the south only a few days later, but there is no means of telling how long they may have paused *en route*. It is certain, however, that birds on migration do not travel at the fantastic speeds which they were thought to do by some older ornithologists, and although their flight may be purposeful and direct it is unlikely that it greatly exceeds the normal flight speed, which is probably between 25–40 miles per hour for most birds. A gaggle of geese tracked by radar for 99 miles was travelling at a ground speed of 35 m.p.h., but allowing for wind the airspeed was only 25 m.p.h.

We do not know how long each individual bird takes on its migration journey, but H. N. Southern, by analysing the records made by people who have noted each year the date of the first big influx, has computed that the main tide of the swallow migration in the spring takes seventy-nine days to cover the two thousand miles from the south of France to the north of Norway. The spread across Europe thus takes place at an average rate of about twenty-five miles per day. There is a tendency for the rate to be slightly faster in the western coastal region and Britain is travelled in just over a fortnight.

We have spoken of the "tide" of migration and the spread is not, of course, the slow moving forward of a great concentrated mass of birds, but is a succession of waves, each wave probably leaving the winter quarters later than the one before and going a little farther.

The British Isles, because of their position on the edge of the Continent and the temperate climate, are very well placed for the study of migration. In the spring they are visited by many species which stay to nest but leave again before the cold weather comes. In the autumn, on the other hand, many birds, hardier than the summer visitors, go there to escape the rigours of winter in North and East Europe. Some of these, such as redwings and fieldfares, and many of the ducks and geese, are birds which are seen there only in the winter; but chaffinches, starlings, rooks, skylarks, and many others, also travel from the Continent in the winter and increase the native population. Many other birds pass through Great Britain on their way north in the spring and again going south in autumn.

Britain is in the path of streams of migra-

Glaucous gull, winter visitor to Britain.

Migrant swallows perching on telegraph wires.

tion from three main directions. The greatest passage is from the north-east, direct across the sea from Scandinavia and North Russia. The birds which come by this route reach land in Shetland and down the east coast of Britain. In the south-east, between the Wash and Dungeness, another great stream comes eastwards across the North Sea from Holland, Denmark, the Baltic, and central Europe. The combined migrations from the east and north-east then pass along the south coast of Britain and across to the north of France.

Waxwings, which in some winters are numerous.

Although some Scandinavian birds go round the north of Scotland and down the west coast of Britain, the main west-coast movements, which are not so heavy as those on the east coast, originate from Greenland, Iceland, and the Faeroes.

In the spring the return migration follows routes similar to those used in the autumn, but in the reverse direction. The spring migration is on a smaller scale than in autumn, when the numbers are swollen by young birds, many of which perish on migration or in their first winter. There is an urgency about the spring migration; the birds are anxious to get to their breeding territories and there is not the lingering on the way which makes autumn migration more apparent.

Not all migration follows the coasts. Many birds which nest in Britain travel overland of necessity, but there is plenty of evidence that passage-migrants often take an inland route, even when they are not forced to do so by adverse weather conditions. Whether some passage-migrants, such as the waders, travel overland by definite routes—one is suspected in a south-westerly direction down the Trent and across to the Severn Valley—or on a broad front is not known for certain, but it is quite probable that both methods are followed.

The return of the migrants in the spring is spread over several months, and the departure in the autumn, when there is less urgency, extends over an even longer period. At the same time as the main migrations, and in the in-between times, other smaller-scale movements are taking place and there is no time in the year when the bird population is completely static.

The spring migration begins about the middle of February, when some of the local migrants begin to move back to their breeding territories. There are return movements, too, of the birds which drifted south, without leaving the country, and of those which emigrated to the milder climate of Ireland. Some of the winter visitors may leave before the

A map showing the general direction of autumn migration of European breeding birds which pass through the British Isles. The three main streams (see text, pages 161-162) are indicated by symbols, as follows:

Birds from Greenland, Iceland, and the Faeroes, including wheatears, redpolls, white wagtails, redwings, white-fronted geese, pink-footed geese, turnstones, purple sandpipers, and golden plover.

Birds from Scandinavia and North Russia, including fieldfares, redwings, bramblings, white-fronted geese, goosanders, and tufted ducks.

Birds from Central Europe, including chaffinches, hooded crows, rooks, jackdaws, sky-larks, starlings, black-headed and common gulls.

163

Chiffchaff, a spring migrant which also occasionally spends the winter in South-west Britain.

end of the month. There may also be reports of very early summer migrants—chiffchaff, wheatear, swallow, and sand-martin are among the birds which sometimes arrive in late February.

All these movements continue, on an increasing scale, in March. More summer residents arrive; by the end of the month the vanguard of about fifteen species has reached the south of England.

April has the greatest number of first arrivals—about thirty species. April also sees the beginning of passage migration. Many migratory birds which nest in Britain also breed farther north or east and pass through on their way. Also passing through are the species, such as bar-tailed godwits and turn-stones, whose breeding grounds lie altogether north of Great Britain. The short summer in the far north means a late nesting season, and some birds will still be passing through the country on their way to the Arctic when British birds have already hatched off their first broods.

May is the peak period of the spring migra-tion; by the end of the first week the earliest arrivals of nearly all summer residents have occurred, and thereafter the main body streams in. Passage migration is at its height. The emigration of winter visitors, which has gone on throughout April, ends in early May.

There is still some inward migration in early June—the first appearance of the marsh-warbler is often in the first week—and the through migration of waders and other birds bound for the far north also goes on.

Almost before the spring migration is over the autumn movement begins. At first it may be the dispersal of non-breeding birds and of the young from early broods rather than true migration. Those birds which nest two or three times in a season often show no interest in their first young when they are busy with the next brood, and may even drive them away.

The earliest movements, whether of adults or of young, do not always have a definite direction and sometimes the bird starts off by travelling north instead of south. A young Sandwich tern, for instance, which was ringed in Fife, was recovered only two days later sixty-five miles to the north, in Aberdeenshire. Another, ringed in Norfolk, travelled over two hundred and eighty miles to the north and reached Angus.

The first of the breeding birds to emigrate are the adult cuckoos—they are not bothered by nest building—which begin to leave early in July. Swifts and some other birds with a very short breeding season also begin to move away in July, and the month sees the beginnings of the passage movement of birds (the waders are the most easily observed) which have completed the short nesting season in North Europe and the Arctic regions.

By the end of August most of the swifts and adult cuckoos have left (the young cuckoos follow later) and individuals of some other summer residents are on the move. But mass emigration does not begin until September. In September, too, immigration from the north and east increases; many birds pass through Britain on their way to South Europe and Africa; others find the British climate warm enough and stay for the winter. September is the best month for watching migration, at inland sewage farms and reservoirs as well as on the coast.

Most of the summer residents have left the British Isles by the middle of October. Birds of the same species seen about—and there are stragglers until November—are more likely to be from farther north or east. October is the peak period of the autumn migration of passage birds and for the arrival of winter visitors, and large-scale movements take place throughout the month and last into early November.

The autumn migration is virtually over by the end of November, but in the winter months there are often movements, more or less on a large scale, dependent on the severity

Sky-lark, a bird which is both a common resident and also a migrant to Britain.

of the weather. In very cold spells enormous movements may be seen, especially of larks, pipits, thrushes, and starlings.

One of the most remarkable aspects of migration is its regularity. The movements outlined above take place each year, and within narrow limits at the same time in each year.

Apart from the annual movements, a few species "irrupt" at fairly regular intervals and invade Britain in much larger numbers than usual. Examples are the crossbill and the waxwing. The crossbill irruptions—the last big one was in 1935—usually occur in the autumn and some of the birds may stay to breed in the following summer. Like the crossbill, the waxwing occurs annually in small numbers, but in some years a mass immigration takes place.

As we have seen, migration does not take place all at once and as a rule there are no mass movements. The observation of migra-

Sedge-warblers, which live mainly on aquatic insects; here the male brings food for the young.

Mistle-thrush, whose migratory movements are not so extensive as those of the song-thrush.

tion on a grand scale is nearly always dependent upon the weather; the best weather for migration is usually the worst for watching it. In fine weather the birds keep to a direct course, possibly at a high altitude, and do not need to alight. Low cloud, rain, and especially fog, bring birds down to a level at which they can be clearly seen. In the autumn south-east gales may hold up migration and blow rare species off their course and bring them to the shores of Great Britain. The effect of wind on migration is not yet clearly understood; birds seem able to migrate equally well with following or adverse winds, in fact they often appear to prefer to fly into a headwind.

The best chances of seeing migration in progress are on the coasts of Britain, especially the east coast, and particularly on headlands and certain small islands. Small islands are good places for watching migration because they are the first resting place after the long sea journey; there is a concentration of birds in a limited area and it is relatively easy to distinguish between migrants and residents.

Bird protection in the
British Isles

BROADLY speaking, the purpose of bird-protection falls into two main divisions. The first is to maintain the richest variety and the maximum numbers in a given area, so far as this is compatible with other reasonable interests. The second is to ensure the survival and spread of the rarer species, some of which are in danger of extermination, others exist in small numbers in a few isolated and remote localities, while yet others, although still not very rare, are steadily diminishing in numbers and must inevitably arouse concern and demand practical action before the danger level is reached. In this second group we must also put any species which may appear and breed for the first time or which reappear after a long period when they were lost to us as breeding species. The avocet, a beautiful black-and-white wader, which is now attempting to re-establish itself as a regular breeding bird in East Anglia after a lapse of over a century, is a good example.

Obviously the protection of rare birds on the "danger list" must be the immediate concern. This is the problem which we must now examine. But the first of the two divisions, the problem of ensuring a rich and varied bird-life in any given area, partially overlaps with this one, and some of the remarks which follow must inevitably pertain to both.

What are the fundamental factors, so far as we can at present judge, having a direct bearing upon the status of birds? The first one which will probably leap to anybody's mind is that of egg-collecting. Now, egg-collecting falls into three main classes: schoolboy collecting, adult collecting of eggs for the cabinet or museum, and the collection of eggs for food. The collecting of eggs by schoolboys need not cause undue alarm; on the whole it has a much greater effect upon the bird-watcher than it does upon the birds: when one is studying seriously the breeding habits of a particular pair of birds and one finds on about the sixth day of incubation that the eggs have been pillaged by some local urchin, one rather naturally wishes to advocate a law which would ensure the imprisonment of all small boys during the months from April to July. Some writers have expressed the view that schoolboy egg-collecting should be condemned on the grounds of cruelty, but lurid and heartrending descriptions of mother blackbirds or thrushes weeping over the nest from which the eggs have been taken by some small and heartless ruffian are figments of the imagination. By far the majority of the smaller birds will begin building a new nest within a few hours or, at most, a day or two of losing either eggs or chicks. A pair of blackbirds will probably rear two and perhaps three broods in a season. If we assume that only two or three chicks are successfully reared in each brood, nevertheless by the end of the summer we shall have seven or eight blackbirds where there were only two in the spring. Now this species is one of the commonest British birds, but, broadly speaking, it certainly does not appear to be increasing. Therefore, it is only logical to suppose that where there are some seven blackbirds at the end of the summer there will be only two left

168

Common tern in breeding plumage, with two very young birds.

Black-headed gull, with young.

Common gulls: the bird in the foreground is in winter plumage.

Herring-gulls: adult and, on the left, an immature bird.

Adult kittiwake in summer plumage, with immature bird in front.

Great black-backed gull.

Common guillemots; behind is the "bridled" variety.

Puffin and young of about one week old.

in the spring. Obviously a very heavy mortality rate occurs in the winter months which is almost certainly related to the shortage of food supply, the much shorter hours of daylight available to the birds for getting food, and the lower temperatures which probably make the birds more hungry than in summer. The argument all boils down to this: with common species it is probable that the greater the rate of increase during the breeding season, the greater will be the mortality in the winter months due to the obviously increased competition for a strictly limited food supply. For this reason alone the robbing of a few clutches of blackbirds' eggs by urchins cannot really be considered to be having the slightest effect upon the numbers of blackbirds as a whole. It may well amount to tens of thousands of eggs taken annually, but is still only a very small fraction of the total eggs laid by the species.

What has been said in the foregoing paragraph should not be misinterpreted. Egg-collecting by youngsters should be discouraged because it is mostly purposeless and futile; it can sometimes interfere very considerably with field-work undertaken by any serious bird-watcher; and it is not impossible that as the egg-collecting child grows up he may develop the selfish and anti-social form of kleptomania which will turn him into an adult egg-collector of the worst order.

So much for predatory youngsters. A much more serious problem arises when we turn to the activities of adult egg-collectors. But even here it is important that we should keep a sense of perspective and avoid being swept away on a tidal wave of our own prejudices. All the forms of collecting in this class are not either selfish or futile; indeed, some serve progressive ends; furthermore, undertaken with common sense and discrimination by responsible, knowledgeable persons, such activities need not adversely affect the numerical status of wild birds. Only an individual with a mind either warped beyond redemption or ignorant beyond conception would assert that no contribution has been made to the science of ornithology by the collecting of eggs. Obviously it is highly desirable, or even imperative, that the large public museums should have available adequate collections which may be referred to by serious students. But, except in the case of the rarer species, such demands could be met without having any noticeable effect on the bird population. With the rarest birds, of course, where the taking of even a single egg may result in a significant and calculable decrease in the total number of young reared, even the scientific and educational claims of a museum clearly have no justification. On the whole, those in charge of the larger museums are well aware of these distinctions; any real threat from this quarter (if it exists at all) would probably come from the curator of a small museum, who would not necessarily have any working knowledge of birds and who might allow ambition to run away with him.

Most of the collecting of eggs destined for the cabinet, however, has no connexion with museums. It must be admitted that some solid scientific achievements have been made by individual collectors; but at the same time it can be said with equal justice that the advances made are infinitesimal by comparison with the effort involved. This brings us face to face with the fundamental issue

Kite, once a common British bird, now rare.

Blackbird, very common near human dwellings and in woods and hedgerows.

dividing the majority of egg-collectors and the bird-protectionists. There are in Britain today a certain number of collectors who do not appear to have the slightest moral scruples in committing acts which are not only illegal but which are ethically about on a par with the activities of a common pickpocket. For instance, the kite, less than two centuries ago a bird familiar almost throughout Britain, is now reduced to a remnant of some six or seven pairs, which nest in a remote part of Wales. Yet in the last few years, in spite of precautions, at least three clutches of kites' eggs have been taken by collectors. Between forty and fifty pairs of that delightful little wader, the red-necked phalarope, nest annually in the whole of Britain; yet in 1948 all the eggs of five pairs nesting in one small area were robbed, and another colony of some seven pairs was also raided and several clutches were taken.

There are about thirty species at present nesting in Britain which can be classed as rare or very rare. These include such birds as the bearded tit, the marsh-harrier, the dotterel, the kite, the red-necked phalarope, the avocet and the golden eagle. Unfortunately, it is the rarer species which are harried by the type of collector who is only anxious to enrich his own cabinets. The scarcer the species becomes, the fewer the eggs that are laid, the greater the latter become as a prize for the cabinet drawer; it is a vicious circle which, unchecked, could only lead to extermination.

The taking of eggs of wild birds for food is a problem which has been accentuated by the general scarcity of food and rationing. It would be neither possible nor desirable to argue all the pros and cons of the matter in this chapter.

Another factor which may be considered to have an effect upon the status of birds lies in the collection of specimens. Here again it can be said with reasonable certainty that in the case of rare species any inroad into the stock will at least prevent a desirable increase and may very well lead to a decrease and ultimate extermination. If the issue in the case of rarer birds is scarcely debatable, the same cannot be said for commoner species. Again we must consider carefully the claims of the museums, the serious research worker and so forth. But even if it is admitted that serious work of scientific value is being achieved by obtaining and comparing bird

Glossy ibis, occasional autumn and spring visitor from South Europe.

skins, the fact remains that a good deal of this "research" is open to grave suspicion. Genuine scientific interests could and should be met by a competent body appointed to assess claims on their merits and to grant licences accordingly; it is, of course, true that no body of individuals, however competent, can be infallible, but on the whole they are better able to assess the facts of any case than the individual who is, rather naturally, generally biased in his own favour.

Sporting interests also affect the status of birds, although to what extent it is not always easy to say. On the whole, legitimate sport in Britain probably has little or no effect on the general status of any birds. Thus the decrease of wildfowl is much more likely to be attributable to adverse circumstances at the breeding-grounds, coupled with the general draining of marshlands, than to the sportsman's activities in the shooting season. On the other hand, many sportsmen who have rightly attacked some of the more sentimental protectionists on the grounds of intolerance bred of ignorance often lay themselves open to these very same charges. The number of birds which still find their way on to keepers' gibbets is legion. Hawks and owls suffer most. Why a keeper should shoot a barn-owl, which subsists largely on rats which will take a tremendous toll of eggs, is beyond all

Cock pied flycatcher perching.

understanding. Yet the senseless massacre continues. Marsh-harriers, of which species only about four or five pairs nest annually in Britain, are still shot in East Anglia. The deplorable slaughter of merlins and golden eagles on the grouse moors are other examples. Within reason it is logical to suppose that preying birds may have a beneficial effect, as it is evident that on the whole they are more likely to take diseased birds.

It has been impossible to cover within the scope of this chapter all the factors affecting the status of wild birds. But one major factor must be mentioned, because, on the whole, it has probably had a greater effect than all the others put together. This is the question of environment. You cannot hope to maintain the numbers of a given species of bird if you start altering its ideal habitat. Certain birds, for example, such as the great and blue tits, the pied flycatcher and the redstart, require holes to breed in. Ancient deciduous woodlands are, therefore, on the whole highly favourable to them. But what happens if (as is indeed happening all over England today) this old timber is cleared and the land turned over to agriculture or made into an aerodrome or planted with regimented soft woods? The answer is quite clear: these hole-nesting birds will be eliminated from the area, at least in the breeding season, unless nest-boxes are provided.

Let us summarize briefly some of the more important factors adverse to wild birds.

Agricultural activities. Better drainage generally, eliminating small areas of rushy ground where the odd pair or two of snipe used to breed, the drier pasture-lands which adversely affect the breeding of lapwings (the young chicks thrive in moister areas); the clearing of hedgerows and replacement by wire fences, a procedure which is certainly affecting the available breeding sites for hedge-nesting birds in many areas; the complete clearance of the few remaining areas of reed-grown fenland, with the consequent *extermination* in the area of such uncommon species as marsh-harriers, bitterns and perhaps

172

Marsh-harrier, which has just alighted on its nest.

Avocets, waders which after more than a century have bred regularly in East Anglia since 1946.

bearded tits, to say nothing of commoner birds, such as many species of ducks, reed-warblers, and so on.

Forestry activities. Wholesale clearance of deciduous woodlands. The planting of conifers, which are on the whole quite unsuitable to most woodland birds, particularly in the breeding season. Furthermore, much of this narrow-leaved afforestation is being carried out on heathlands. In East Anglia the stone-curlew is certainly being further reduced in numbers by activity of this kind.

Sporting activities. A lot of unfair criticism has been levelled at sportsmen. The passing of the old shooting estates, properly maintained and with vermin kept under control, is, on the whole, a loss to bird-protection. If it is true that many rare birds of prey, such as harriers, were slaughtered, the area patrolled by a hard-working gamekeeper was at least properly safeguarded from general molestation, while the numbers of carrion-crows, rats,

stoats, and grey squirrels were at least kept within reasonable bounds.

Egg-collecting. The activities of collectors can certainly be detrimental. The taking of eggs of such rare local species as the marsh-harrier, Montagu's harrier, bittern, bearded tit, kite, dotterel, hobby, golden eagle, and Dartford warbler—this sort of collecting is purely acquisitive; it serves no scientific purposes, and as the collectors know quite well how parlous is the position of some of the species which they are raping, their actions cannot be too heartily condemned. It is important to bear in mind, however, that many egg-collectors are vigorously opposed to the taking of the eggs of rarities (though sometimes, it must be admitted, only after they themselves have acquired a single clutch of each species concerned). It is doubtful if the collecting of eggs of commoner birds, on the scale on which it is practised today, has any noticeable effect on their status. Schoolboy egg-collecting may have an effect in an urban area (though it is probably completely masked by the activities of cats), but in rural areas the effect is probably nil.

Urbanization. The spread of cities obviously affects some birds detrimentally. It is true that sometimes parks are called "sanctuaries" and the birds therein are nominally protected. But the parks are usually too formal to encourage a reasonable variety of bird-life.

Services' requirements. Often the reservation of an area for military requirements is directly beneficial to the bird life of the area by preventing public access. Sometimes, however, it can be disastrous. Tank manoeuvres have ruined more than one famous haunt of the Dartford warbler.

Bird-photographers are not always helpful to the birds, nor are some of the activities of "rubber-necking" bird-watchers.

Golden eagle, now an established breeder only in Scotland.

What are the remedies? How can we ensure that bird life shall not only continue to flourish but be enriched? Let us bear in mind that an ideal solution is not feasible. All we can hope to do is to preserve small representative areas and we must continue to educate the general public into a proper appreciation of the issues involved. Birds are pleasant things to have around us and, on the whole, people are not unresponsive to them. More can be achieved through education than through legislation. A hundred times as many clutches are probably destroyed by the activities of hedgers and ditchers as would ever be taken by collectors. At present the majority of British birds and their eggs are nominally protected. Each county and county borough, however, has its separate

Bittern, re-established as a British breeder in 1911, seen removing egg-shell from nest.

Lapwing on an unusually wet and bulky nest in a flooded marsh.

orders, and many curious and ridiculous anomalies have resulted.

What is the remedy? Obviously, there is need for a completely new and straightforward piece of legislation which can at least have some hope of achieving what it sets out to do. The obvious basic idea would be to put all birds and their eggs on the protected list throughout Britain. Certain birds, such as the carrion-crow and house-sparrow and wood-pigeon, would be put on a special list and would not be protected at all. This "black list" would be altered from time to time and might be altered slightly from region to region. In this way all the birds which could legally be destroyed would be common ones and, therefore, would be known by the majority of the public and members of

Dartford warbler perched on a furze bush (above),
and (below) *cock common redstart.*

the police force. At the present moment a gamekeeper shooting an osprey can probably honestly plead that he did not know it was an osprey. It would be difficult for somebody shooting an osprey to claim that he thought it was a carrion-crow or wood-pigeon. Of course, if all birds are put on a protected list, a clause must be inserted in the legislation to allow for the taking of eggs or specimens for educational or scientific purposes. There must be an "open" season for game-birds.

In the meantime, conservation is making progress and the individual can do much to help it. A good lead has recently been given by the State in the establishment of the Nature Conservancy, which will ultimately become a great power for good, but for many years to come it would seem that the major burden of bird protection must continue to fall upon the Royal Society for the Protection of Birds. The Society's activities are only limited by the amount of support it receives. It is extremely active in education in schools; it also administers a number of very fine bird sanctuaries and is acquiring new ones; it encourages the safe breeding of a number of rare species through a system of bounties. There are also many local bodies doing splendid work; the individual should certainly support any such body which may be functioning in his area. He can also do much by trying a sympathetic approach to teachers and gamekeepers and similar people who, once interest is aroused, can do much to help. He can encourage the bird life in his own garden or estate by putting up nesting-boxes, planting suitable bushes and hedges, and by leaving rough patches of waste ground.

Bird protection is a big and complex problem. It is important to try to see it steadily and to see it whole. Avoid hysterics like the plague. If a species of bird is harmful, why should it not be controlled? Few people are unduly concerned about the perpetual massacre of rats, often in extremely painful ways. If rabbits are shot to provide human food, why not ducks so long as the breeding population is not reduced?

178

Eggs, their colours and markings

EGGS vary widely, particularly in colouring and number laid, not merely between those of different species but even from clutch to clutch of birds of the same species. For example, the eggs of the mistle-thrush may be of any shade from brownish-white to bluish-green; and the clutch, though usually consisting of four eggs, has been observed to contain as few as three and as many as six. Markings, such as blotching, streaking, or mottling, also vary widely from egg to egg. It is therefore impossible to give exact details of the eggs of any particular bird, though enough general description can be given to assist greatly in identification. In the following pages, as an aid to identification, such general description of the eggs, of the usual numbers, and of the minimum and maximum numbers observed in a clutch (in brackets), is given for birds which breed in Great Britain.

CROWS AND THE STARLING

BIRD	EGG COLOUR	NUMBER
Raven	blue to green, blotched brown and black	4-6 (2-7)
Hooded crow	blue to green, blotched umber-brown	4-6 (4-7)
Carrion-crow	ditto: commonly paler	4-5 (4-7)
Rook	ditto: more uniformly blotched ash-grey and brown	3-5 (3-9)
Jackdaw	ditto: bluer, less blotched black and brown	4-6 (2-9)
Magpie	blue-, yellow-, or grey-green closely mottled brown and ash	5-8 (5-10)
Jay	dull green, finely mottled olive spots, black hair-line big end	5-6 (3-8)
Chough	white or cream, thickly mottled brown and ash	3-6 (2-7)
Starling	very pale glossed blue	5-7 (4-9)

FINCHES, BUNTINGS, AND SPARROWS

BIRD	EGG COLOUR	NUMBER
Hawfinch	pale bluish to grey-green, with bold blackish-brown spots and streaks	4-6 (2-7)
Greenfinch	whitish or pale greenish-blue, with red-brown spots and streaks and pale violet shell-marks	4-6 (3-8)
Goldfinch	bluish-white with few red-brown spots and streaks and ashy shell-marks	5-6 (3-7)
Siskin	blue with pale reddish spots and streaks	3-5 (2-6)
Lesser redpoll	deep blue with light brown spots and streaks	4-5 (3-7)
Twite	blue with few bold red-brown spots and streaks	5-6 (4-7)
Linnet	paler blue with purple-red spots	4-6 (4-7)
Bullfinch	green-blue with few purple-brown spots	4-5 (4-7)
Crossbill	greenish-white with few purple-red spots and streaks	4 (2-5)
Chaffinch	greenish-blue to stone with purple-brown spots and streaks	4-5 (4-8)
Corn-bunting	greyish-white to light brown with bold brownish-black wavy lines	3-5 (1-6)
Yellow bunting	whitish to pale brownish-red with dark-brown hair-lines	3-4 (2-6)
Cirl-bunting	bluish or greenish with black streaks and hair-lines	3-4 (2-5)

Nest and eggs of reed-bunting in a clump of marsh grass.

BIRD	EGG COLOUR	NUMBER
Reed-bunting	brownish-olive with few blackish-brown streaks and spots and grey shell-marks	4-5 (4-6)
Snow-bunting	whitish with reddish and blackish blotches and spots, violet shell-marks	4-6 (4-8)
House-sparrow	greyish-white, uniformly spotted dark grey and brown: one egg usually lighter than rest	3-5 (3-8)

BIRD	EGG COLOUR	NUMBER
Tree-sparrow	ditto, but smaller, browner and more finely spotted	4-6 (4-9)

LARKS, PIPITS, AND WAGTAILS

BIRD	EGG COLOUR	NUMBER
Wood-lark	greyish-white with brownish freckles and violet-grey shell-marks	3-4 (3-6)
Sky-lark	greyish-white, uniform olive or brown freckling	3-4 (3-7)
Tree-pipit	variable: usually red, brown or grey, uniformly speckled	4-6 (4-8)

Blackbird's nest with a normal clutch of four eggs.

BIRD	EGG COLOUR	NUMBER
Meadow-pipit	variable: brown or grey, mottled and marbled	3-6
Rock-pipit	greyish-white, thickly spotted olive-brown or ashy-grey	4-5 (2-6)
Blue-headed wagtail	uniform reddish-brown	5-6 (5-7)
Yellow wagtail	ditto	6 (4-8)
Grey wagtail	buff, faintly marbled greyish-brown	4-6 (3-7)

BIRD	EGG COLOUR	NUMBER
Pied wagtail	greyish or bluish-white with even grey-brown or grey spots	5-6 (3-7)

TREE-CREEPER, NUTHATCH, TITS, AND GOLDCREST

BIRD	EGG COLOUR	NUMBER
Tree-creeper	White with zone of red-brown spots, reddish-violet shell-marks	6 (3-9)
Nuthatch	White with red-brown spots and few violet shell-marks	6-11 (4-13)

Bittern's "platform" nest and eggs.

The closely woven nest of a blackcap.

Long-eared owl's nest on ground.

BIRD	EGG COLOUR	NUMBER
Great tit	white with red-brown blotches	5-11 (5-18)
Blue tit	white with pale chestnut speckles	7-14 (5-24)
Coal-tit	white with red-brown spots	7-11 (5-14)
Crested tit	as Tree-creeper, but without shell-marks	5-6 (5-8)
Marsh-tit	white with few red-brown spots	7-8 (5-11)
Willow-tit	ditto, but often more richly marked	8-9 (5-13)
Long-tailed tit	ditto, sometimes unmarked	8-12 (5-20)
Bearded tit	white, with fine liver-brown markings	5-7 (5-12)
Goldcrest	whitish or ochreous with zone of fine brown spots	7-10 (7-13)

RED-BACKED SHRIKE AND FLYCATCHERS

Red-backed shrike	variable: from cream through pale green to pink or brown	5-6 (5-7)

182

Lapwing's nest. Compare the unusual one on page 177.

Redstart's loosely built nest in a rock cranny.

Carrion-crow's nest: there are usually four or five eggs.

BIRD	EGG COLOUR	NUMBER
Spotted flycatcher	green-grey with red-brown spots or cap	4-5 (4-9)
Pied flycatcher	pale blue	4-7 (4-10)

WARBLERS

Chiffchaff	glossy white with purple-brown spots and speckles	6 (4-7)
Willow-warbler	variable: pale red freckles, pale red-brown blotches, or dark brown spots	6-7 (3-9)
Wood-warbler	white with dark red-brown spots and speckles	6-7 (4-8)
Grasshopper-warbler	cream with dense brown-red spots	6 (4-7)
Reed-warbler	greenish-white with dark olive and ash-grey blotching and marbling	4 (3-6)
Marsh-warbler	bluish or green-white with few bold olive-brown spots and blotches and ashy shell-marks	4-5 (3-6)
Sedge-warbler	dense ochre speckling	5-6 (3-8)
Garden-warbler	white, yellow or green with pale olive and brown blotches and spots	4-5 (3-7)

183

BIRD	EGG COLOUR	NUMBER
Blackcap	ditto: often smaller and less glossy	5 (3-6)
Whitethroat	variable: usually green-ish or stone with ochre and ashy speckling	4-5 (3-7)
Lesser whitethroat	creamy-white with brown and grey shell-marks	4-6 (3-7)
Dartford warbler	whitish or greenish with fine olive-brown or ash-grey spots	3-4 (3-6)

THRUSHES, CHATS, ACCENTOR, WREN, AND DIPPER

Mistle-thrush	creamy to green-blue with brown spots and blotches and lilac shell-marks	4 (3-6)
Song-thrush	blue with few black spots	4-5 (3-9)
Ring-ouzel	blue-green with few red-brown blotches	4 (3-6)
Blackbird	blue-green with red-brown freckles	4-5 (3-9)
Wheatear	pale blue	6 (3-8)
Whinchat	blue-green with rust-brown speckles	5-6 (4-7)
Stonechat	ditto: but paler and greener	5-6 (3-8)
Redstart	pale blue	6 (5-7)
Black redstart	glossy white	4-6

Robin's nest in an old watering-can.

BIRD	EGG COLOUR	NUMBER
Nightingale	speckled olive-green or olive-brown	4-5 (3-7)
Robin	white with dense reddish freckles	5-6 (3-10)
Hedge-sparrow	deep blue	4-5 (3-6)
Wren	white with brown-red spots	5-6 (3-16)
Dipper	pure white	5 (3-7)

SWALLOWS, SWIFT, AND NIGHTJAR

Swallow	white with red-brown spots and ashy shell-marks	4-5 (3-8)
House-martin	white	4-5 (2-6)
Sand-martin	white	4-5 (3-7)
Swift	dull white	3 (2-4)
Nightjar	greyish-white to cream with yellow-brown blotching and marbling	2 (2-4)

KINGFISHER, WOODPECKERS, AND CUCKOO

Kingfisher	glossy white	6-7 (4-10)
Green woodpecker	white	5-7 (4-11)
Great spotted woodpecker	glossy white	4-7 (3-8)
Lesser spotted woodpecker	ditto	4-6 (3-8)
Wryneck	dull white	7-10 (5-14)
Cuckoo	variable: resembling fosterer's, but with brown and grey spots and blotches	1 in each nest

OWLS

Little owl	white	3-5 (2-8)
Long-eared owl	ditto	4-5 (3-8)
Short-eared owl	dull white	4-8 (3-13)
Tawny owl	white	2-4 (1-8)
Barn-owl	ditto	4-7 (3-11)

BIRDS OF PREY

Peregrine falcon	red-brown	3-4 (1-6)
Hobby	red-brown stippling	3 (2-4)
Merlin	purple-brown stippling	4 (3-6)

184

Razorbill and two-day-old chick.

Pair of black grouse: blackcock in front, greyhen behind.

Adult red grouse and young as they appear about 20 August.

Cock and hen common partridges by a clump of campion.

Pair of red-legged partridges with brood of young.

Moorhen and young by a white water-lily.

Coot and young at the nest.

BIRD	EGG COLOUR	NUMBER
Kestrel	white with red-brown blotching and washing	4-5 (4-9)
Golden eagle	white, or with red-brown and ash-grey flecks and spots	2 (1-4)
Common buzzard	white with red or brown blotches	2-3 (1-6)
Marsh-harrier	bluish-white	4-5 (3-8)
Montagu's harrier	pale blue-white or white	4-5 (3-10)
Hen-harrier	bluish-white	4-5 (3-8)
Sparrow-hawk	bluish-white with dark-brown blotches, spots, and streaks	4-5 (3-10)
Kite	white	2-3 (2-4)

HERON AND BITTERN

BIRD	EGG COLOUR	NUMBER
Heron	green-blue	3-5 (2-7)
Bittern	olive-brown	4-6 (3-7)

MUTE SWAN, GEESE, AND SHELD-DUCK

BIRD	EGG COLOUR	NUMBER
Mute swan	white, tinted grey or blue-green	5-7 (4-12)
Grey lag-goose	creamy-white	4-6 (3-8)
Canada goose	ditto	5-6 (2-11)
Sheld-duck	ditto	8-16 (8-20)

DUCKS

BIRD	EGG COLOUR	NUMBER
Mallard	grey-green or buff-green	10-12 (7-16)
Gadwall	buff-cream	8-12 (7-16)
Teal	pale stone to pale green-buff	8-10 (8-16)
Garganey	creamy-buff	7-12 (7-14)
Wigeon	cream or buff	7-8 (6-10)
Pintail	cream to yellow-green or bluish	7-9 (6-12)
Shoveler	tinged green or buff	8-12 (7-14)
Pochard	green-grey	6-11 (6-15)
Tufted duck	ditto	6-14 (6-18)
Eider	olive to buff or ivory	4-6 (3-10)
Common scoter	cream or buff	5-7 (5-13)
Goosander	creamy-white	7-13 (7-15)
Red-breasted merganser	stone to green-buff	7-12 (7-17)

CORMORANTS, GANNET, PETRELS, AND MANX SHEARWATER

BIRD	EGG COLOUR	NUMBER
Cormorant	blue with chalk-white deposit	4 (3-6)
Shag	ditto	3 (2-6)
Gannet	blue-white	1 (1-2)
Storm-petrel	white with few brown speckles	1 (1-2)
Fork-tailed petrel	white with few sandy speckles	1
Manx shearwater	white	1
Fulmar	white	1 (1-2)

GREBES AND DIVERS

BIRD	EGG COLOUR	NUMBER
Great crested grebe	chalk-white, stained to buff	3-4 (3-9)
Slavonian grebe	ditto, stained dark	4 (3-6)
Black-necked grebe	ditto ditto	3-4 (2-5)
Little grebe	ditto ditto	4-6 (2-10)
Black-throated diver	green-olive to dark umber with black spots	2 (1-3)
Red-throated diver	olive-green, yellow or brown with black-brown spots and blotchs	2 (1-3)

PIGEONS

BIRD	EGG COLOUR	NUMBER
Wood-pigeon	glossed white	2 (1-3)
Stock-dove	white tinged cream	2 (1-4)
Rock-dove	glossed white	2 (1-2)
Turtle-dove	ditto	2 (1-3)

Eider duck's nest surrounded by down.

185

Above: *Redshank's eggs.*

Left: *Puffin's untidy nest and single egg.*

Eggs of the black guillemot, which builds no nest.

Collection of Sandwich terns' eggs.

BIRD	EGG COLOUR	NUMBER

WADERS I
CURLEW AND SANDPIPER

Curlew	green-brown with brown spots	4 (3-6)
Whimbrel	ditto, with dark spots	4 (3-5)
Dunlin	green-buff with brown spots and blotches	4 (2-6)
Common sandpiper	grey-buff with chestnut markings	4 (3-5)
Redshank	buff with brown spots	4 (3-5)
Greenshank	buff with red-brown blotches and streaks	4 (3-5)

WADERS II
SNIPE AND PLOVERS

Woodcock	buff with brown spots	4 (3-6)
Snipe	olive with brown spots	4 (3-6)
Red-necked phalarope	buff with dark spots	4 (3-5)
Ringed plover	grey with dark spots	4 (3-5)
Golden plover	buff with dark brown blotches	4 (3-4)
Dotterel	buff with black-brown blotches	3 (2-4)
Lapwing	buff with black spots	4 (3-5)
Oyster-catcher	stone-buff with dark brown spots and blotches	3 (2-5)
Stone-curlew	stone with dark brown spots	2-3

TERNS, GULLS, AND SKUAS

Sandwich tern	buff with black-brown spots	2 (1-3)
Roseate tern	buff with reddish spots and blotches	2 (1-3)
Common tern	stone with dark brown spots and blotches	3 (2-4)

186

Above: *Woodcock's eggs.*

Right: *Nesting hollow and eggs of common tern.*

BIRD	EGG COLOUR	NUMBER
Arctic tern	ditto	2 (1-4)
Little tern	ditto	2 (2-4)
Black-headed gull	stone-buff with dark-brown spots	3 (2-4)
Common gull	olive with brown blotches	3 (2-4)
Herring-gull	olive-brown with dark-brown spots	3 (2-5)
Lesser black-backed gull	ditto	3 (2-4)
Great black-backed gull	stone with dark-brown spots	3 (2-5)
Kittiwake	stone with brown blotches	2 (1-3)
Great skua	variable: usually brown or olive-brown with similar blotchings	2 (1-4)
Arctic skua	variable: usually olive with darker blotchings	2 (1-2)

BIRD	EGG COLOUR	NUMBER
	AUKS	
Razorbill	variable: brown to white with brown or black markings	1 (1-2)
Guillemot	ditto, blue-green, reddish, cream or white, with yellow, red, brown or black markings	1
Black guillemot	whitish with dark-brown and grey	2 (1-3)
Puffin	white, sometimes with brown markings	1 (1-2)
	RAILS	
Corn-crake	pale green-grey to pale red-brown, with red-brown and ash-grey blotches and spots	6-14 (6-19)
Spotted crake	olive-buff with purple-brown and ashy grey spots and blotches	8-12 (6-15)

Collection of guillemots' eggs, showing the wide variety of shade and markings.

Pheasant's nest and twenty-one eggs—an unusually large clutch.

BIRD	EGG COLOUR	NUMBER	BIRD	EGG COLOUR	NUMBER
Water-rail	paler than corn-crake's	6-11 (5-16)	*Red grouse*	yellow-white heavily blotched with dark or red-brown	6-11 (4-17)
Moorhen	whitish to buff or greenish, tinged with red-brown spots and blue-ash shell-marks	5-11 (2-26)	*Ptarmigan*	ditto, smaller and paler	5-9 (3-17)
Coot	stone with dark-brown speckles and spots	6-9 (6-22)	*Pheasant*	olive-brown	8-15 (7-22)
			Partridge	ditto	9-20 (8-23)

GAME-BIRDS

BIRD	EGG COLOUR	NUMBER	BIRD	EGG COLOUR	NUMBER
Capercaillie	pale yellow with few yellow or red-brown spots and blotches	5-8 (4-18)	*Red-legged partridge*	yellowish with few ochre-red spots and ashy shell-marks	10-16 (7-28)
Black grouse	ditto, smaller	6-10 (5-16)	*Quail*	yellowish-white with dark-brown markings	7-12 (6-18)

Curlews hatching : a chick is about to emerge from the egg on the extreme left.

INDEX

Numbers in italics indicate illustrations

ACKNOWLEDGEMENTS

The publishers acknowledge with thanks permission to reproduce photographs as follows: to Robert Atkinson, pictures on pages 76, 159; R. Beach, 143 (herring-gull); J. Berry, 102 (bean-goose); G. Bird, 46, 60, 67, 85, 86 (long-eared owl), 103, 114, 124, 132 (nestling), 135, 140, 153, 160, 165, 166, 167, 170, 178 (redstart), 182 (bittern), 186, 187; Arthur Brook, 4 (merlin), 15, 23, 25, 27, 35, 38, 39, 43, 55, 77, 80, 90, 98, 108 (eider), 119 (stock-dove), 122, 127, 130, 131, 158, 164, 169, 175; Ralph Chislett, 54, 120, 123 (hen), 128; D. N. Dalton, 136; M. D. England, 134; Guy B. Farrar, 121, 123 (cock), 139; C. A. Gibson-Hill, 29, 112, 137, 148; J. Hoskin, 100 (white-fronted goose); Eric Hosking, 11, 12, 13, 14, 19, 30, 31, 37, 41, 42, 45, 47, 50, 56, 57, 58, 59, 61, 62, 63, 65, 68, 69, 71, 72, 75, 78, 79, 81, 82, 83, 84, 86 (short-eared owl), 87, 92, 94, 95, 106, 110, 111, 116, 117, 129, 132 (adult birds), 133, 138, 143 (lesser black-backed gull), 144, 145, 147, 150, 151, 154, 172, 173, 176, 181, 182 (black-cap, owl), 183, 184, 188, 189; National Audubon Society, 109 (surf-scoter), 171; Alasdair Alpin Mac-Gregor, 185; H. Morrey Salmon, 28, 105, 113, 118; Richard Perry, 146; Oliver Pike, 102 (Canada geese), 104, 108 (gadwall), 109 (gadwall), 115; S. C. Porter, 107, 126, 155, 163 (waxwings), 177; J. D. Rattar, 141, 161; H. N. Southern, 93; C. W. Teager, 70; A. R. Thompson, 44, 100 (barnacle-goose), 101 (grey lag-goose), 180; Ian M. Thomson, 40, 174; and G. K. Yeates, 26, 36, 49, 51, 52, 66, 73, 96, 97, 101 (whooper swan), 125, 178 (Dartford warbler).